D0312152

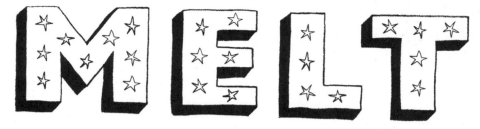

MELT

ICE CREAM SENSATIONS TO MAKE AT HOME

CLAIRE KELSEY

PHOTOGRAPHY BY EMILY DENNISON
DESIGNED BY ANITA MANGAN

First published in Great Britain in 2013 by Simon & Schuster UK Ltd
A CBS COMPANY

Copyright © Claire Kelsey, 2013

This book is copyright under the Berne Convention.
No reproduction without permission. All rights reserved.

The right of Claire Kelsey to be identified as the author of this work
has been asserted by her in accordance with sections 77 and 78 of the
Copyright, Designs and Patents Act, 1988.

10 9 8 7 6 5 4 3 2 1

SIMON & SCHUSTER ILLUSTRATED BOOKS
Simon & Schuster UK Ltd
222 Gray's Inn Road
London
WC1X 8HB

www.simonandschuster.co.uk
Simon & Schuster Australia, Sydney
Simon & Schuster India, New Delhi

A CIP catalogue record for this book is available from the British Library.
ISBN: 978–1–47110–191–5

Created by Harris + Wilson
Designed by Anita Mangan
Photographs © Emily Dennison 2013
Illustrations © Abigail Read and Anita Mangan 2013
Printed and bound in China
Colour reproduction by Dot Gradations Ltd, UK

Notes on the recipes:

Both metric and imperial measurements have been given. Use one set
of measurements only and not a mixture of both. Spoon measures are level:
for quick reference, 1 tablespoon = 15 ml, 1 teaspoon = 5 ml.

Preheat ovens before use and cook on the centre shelf unless cooking more
than one item. If using a fan oven, reduce the heat by 10–20°C, but check
with your manufacturer's handbook. Always keep an eye on items that are
baking in an oven – cooking times are for guidance only. Recipes have been
tested and timed using a gas hob; please note that an electric hob will give
different cooking times for thickening custards and so on.

Similarly, the freezing times will vary according to the make and model
of your freezer. Use those given here as a guide.

Use medium-sized eggs throughout, except where specified otherwise.
Use granulated sugar, except where specified otherwise.
Volumes for final ice-cream mix are approximate. For numbers of servings,
1 litre/35 fl oz ice cream serves approximately 4–6 people.

Every effort has been made to ensure that the information contained
in this book is complete and accurate. However, neither the publisher
nor the author is engaged in rendering professional advice or services
to the individual reader. Neither the publisher nor the author accepts
any legal responsibility for the personal injury or other damage or loss
arising from the use or misuse of the information and advice in this book.

CONTENTS

ICE CREAM IS EASY

G inger is a 1997 Ford Transit ice-cream van. It wouldn't be fair to call her an impulse buy, but in December 2009 I decided that, as a catering unit, an ice-cream van might be an interesting prospect.

A week later I had one in my drive with no real business plan. I just knew that the project of making the van my own would involve bringing together the skills of all my talented family and friends, and would be the most fun I'd ever have in the name of work. The general notion, I suspect, was to get me and my mates into summer festivals and take the van to parties. I had no idea that Ginger would take over my work life as a food stylist.

My dad and I sprayed her pink and maroon, then furnished the inside with distressed mirrors and wood – a nod to Parisian cafés that look so inviting – and lined the walls with classic Parisian poster designs.

My friend Nicky was the next to get involved. She was learning the techniques of gilding and signwriting and Ginger became her first proper effort in the purest real gold, with beautiful drop-shadowing. My enduring image of this time is Nicky, roll-up in hand, head cocked to one side, staring at her work with an expression of mild displeasure; but that's because she's a perfectionist.

The name I owe to my buddy Vic, who traded it for a lifetime's supply of ice cream. My friend Stan helped me with the logo designs and font. When I stand back now and look at Ginger, the pride I feel is purely for all the people who made her what she is today.

Ice cream fires my imagination – it's an experimental cook's dream. Cream, sugar and eggs set the stage for any flavour combos you can think up. Let me say that I, maybe like you, hadn't made much ice cream when I started out. I had no ice-cream churns and no catering premises. I had to learn the best methods for freezing ice cream without a churn, in a domestic kitchen, from scratch. That's why, as a novice, you might like trying your hand at some of the 'no churn' recipes, such as Marmalade on Toast or Eccles Cake ice cream. Both scoop just like a churned ice cream and are wickedly tasty, super-smooth and straightforward to make.

For the more confident (I don't always like to have it easy in the kitchen), there are more challenging recipes, such as the English Country Garden Sorbet Pops, or Monkey Gone to Heaven, which will introduce you to some new techniques.

People often ask me what my most unusual flavour is. The one that surprises most customers is XV Olive Oil Ice Cream with Smoked Sea Salt Crystals. If you think about it, the flavour notes of many foods aren't intrinsically savoury or sweet, it's how they're applied. I adore this recipe – olive oil in ice cream is fresh, grassy, almost melony, with a peppery aftertaste.

I hope you enjoy this collection. Whether you're looking for something creamy, fruity, nutty, spicy or boozy, whipping up something to share, or celebrating with an ice-cream cake, you'll find something to inspire you in this book. You'll also discover more exciting ways to serve your scoops, such as Ginger Sling with a Pineapple Heart, which brings sharp, cold sorbet to a warming spiced rice pudding, or Apple Fool with Mincemeat Granita and Honey Crumbs, which plays with contrasting tastes and textures.

A supermodel was once quoted as saying: "Nothing tastes as good as skinny feels." Well, I disagree. My ethos has always been: "If something tastes this good, I'll happily gain a pound to eat it." Not as snappy, but I hope you'll appreciate the sentiment.

WHAT YOU'LL NEED

Here's a list of things I can't go without, and you might find useful to invest in. Nothing too out of the ordinary for someone who knows one end of a wooden spoon from the other. Everything you need to make a frozen masterpiece is probably already right there in your kitchen cupboards.

1. **Electric whisk**
   I can't do without one; they save time and effort. You might prefer just to use elbow grease and a balloon whisk.

2. **Ladle**
   Really useful when making egg-custard bases.

3. **Wooden spoon**
   Of course! Every good kitchen's got one already, right?

4. **Balloon whisk**
   Essential, but doesn't have to be fancy.

5. **Hand blender**
   For emulsifying, and making mixtures as smooth as possible.

6. **Jug**
   For measuring and pouring. I prefer the cheaper, transparent plastic ones.

7. **Saucepans**
   Heavy-bottomed or cast-iron ones are best for making custards as they disperse heat evenly. Also, cast-iron pans have a light-coloured base, which is good for watching the changing colour of caramel.

8. **Fine sieve**
   Anything you can strain rice through is okay.

9. **Bowls**
   No need for cutesy ceramic ones, although they do look pretty. I prefer to have several sizes of lightweight plastic ones, as there's a lot of lifting and scraping.

10. **Tubs for freezing**
    Most recipes make 1-2 litres (35-70 fl oz).

11. **Microplane® grater**
    The best thing for zesting and grating things like ginger. A good investment.

12. **Spatula (aka Child Cheater)**
    Silicone ones leave the smallest amount of precious mixture around the sides of your bowl.

CHURNING ICE CREAM

Why do we churn ice cream? How does it work? Simply, the churn keeps your mixture moving while it freezes, thereby controlling the formation of ice. If you freeze a tub of ice cream without churning, you get an ice block. Keep the mix in motion and the consistency will be soft and smooth. There are a lot of different ways to churn, and I've tried them all for you.

 Many of the ice creams in this book don't need churning at all. These are marked with a 'no churn' symbol.

PRE-FREEZE ICE-CREAM MACHINES

These are the most easily found ice-cream makers. They do all the churning work for you, but you must put the barrel in the freezer the night before you want to make ice cream. So the downside is that there's no spontaneity. And, secondly, you can only make one batch in a 24-hour period.

ICE-CREAM MACHINES WITH INBUILT COMPRESSOR

These are the daddy of ice-cream churning. While even the best domestic machines make only up to 1 litre (35 fl oz) of mix at a time (before having to re-freeze the drum), these can make as much ice cream as you need on the spot relatively quickly and easily. A compressor inside the machine freezes, while a motor turns the paddle.

STIR-FREEZING

If you don't have an ice-cream maker, this is the best method to use. A lot of people are put off ice-cream making because of the stress put on controlling the 'formation of ice crystals', as if it's a mysterious dark art practised only by those with a special ice-cream licence. It won't be the worst disaster if your ice cream develops the odd icy bit. You'll get a decent result from this method, especially with ice creams with a high sugar content, such as my Peanut Butter and Salted Caramel recipe (page 75).

Pop your mix in a lidded tub, whack it in the freezer, then remember to go back and give it a good stir after 40 minutes, then every half-hour or so until the mixture is firm and smooth. Depending on the temperature of your freezer, which should be at least -18°C (0°F), the full time to stir-freeze a litre of ice cream might be around four hours. It's not as if you have to sit staring at the freezer with a stopwatch – just don't go out and forget about it.

For the best result, put the wet mix in a larger container with a bigger surface area as it will be quicker to freeze. For a lighter, smoother texture, use a hand blender for the last stir, which will blitz the ice crystals. (Stir in any sprinkles or other nuggets after this point.)

HAND-OPERATED BARREL WITH PADDLE

The plus point is that these are cheap and available online, but they're messy and time-consuming and rely on using ice and salt to freeze.

When ice and salt are put together in the barrel – you need roughly 4 kg (9 lb) of ice per 2 kg (4 lb 8 oz) of salt – it will get very cold. Salt melts ice, and in doing so draws heat energy from around it. Temperatures can drop as low as -21°C (-6°F). Mine didn't get this low: my thermometer read -17°C (1°F) at its lowest and didn't hold long enough to get the ice cream hard enough. I think I tried to freeze too much – if you want to churn more than 400–500 ml (14–18 fl oz), this method isn't for you. I sat turning the little handle for an hour, wondering which animal it would be easiest to train to do it for me (a hamster on his wheel, attached to the paddle, in case you're wondering).

However, the barrel I use is a lovely piece of design and I'm glad I picked it up. I found it in a charity shop – and I almost mistook it for a salad spinner. I'm sure it's got other uses.

CATCH! BALL-CHURNING

A ball churn is a sphere that holds ice and salt, into which you deposit your ice-cream mix. This relies again on the cooling effects of ice and salt, but the motion comes from flinging it about. Brilliant if you're watching your weight; the calories you burn may well equal those you're putting back in. Fun, especially for a picnic. Before I realised these can easily be purchased online, I tried to make one from a hamster's exercise ball …

I don't use gyms for a few reasons, mostly because I don't see sense in using electricity to power machines that burn energy themselves. I'd rather run outside. If we're to burn excess calories on the thousands of treadmills and cross-trainers across the country, wouldn't it be better the other way around? Our efforts could power other things, like city-centre lights, for example. Which neatly leads me on to …

PEDAL POWER

If you can hook a plastic or other lightweight barrel to the front of a cycle so that it rests on the front wheel, you've got a brilliant and leisurely way to churn. Fix it so that the barrel can move independently from the part that holds it, allowing it to spin.

We took an old metal biscuit barrel and an old-fashioned stationary exercise bike. We put hooks at each end of the barrel, which was then attached to the bike using the handlebar section from another old cycle. The barrel sits between the handlebar supports, resting against the front wheel of the exercise bike. The "yoke" (which runs from the handlebars to the centre of the front wheel) attaches between the handlebars of the exercise bike.

I'm aware that this doesn't sound like the easiest thing in the world. My dad helped me develop it, and I knew he'd get carried away with his engineering skills. (He used to do the same with my school art projects as a kid; my Viking long boats weren't made from an old squeezy bottle if he could help it.) The principle is easy enough to understand, though. Once the barrel is in place, fill it with ice and salt and a pouch of custard, and go for a spin.

DRY ICE

Dry ice is the solid form of carbon dioxide, which is sold in small pellets. It can be bought online for a reasonable price – low enough that you might think about using it for a party. You must make sure the dry ice you buy is food-grade quality.

The beauty of dry ice is that you can store it in a cool place in the insulated box it arrives in. It's safe to handle as long as you don't expose your skin to it for too long. Its temperature is -78°C (-108°F): don't hold it without gloves – if you do, you'll get a burn similar to a heat burn. Wear safety goggles to protect your eyes.

To freeze ice cream with dry ice, wait until the mixture is cold, lightly crush the pellets in a pestle and mortar, then spoon the powder into the mixture as you stir. It can be hard to judge how much you need (the powder will smoke up the bowl), but you'll feel the mixture stiffen. Don't try the ice cream just yet – wait a few minutes until it has 'warmed up' enough not to burn you.

You can't store leftover dry ice for long; it will disappear into the atmosphere after a couple of days. If you don't have 20 litres of ice cream to make, then have fun with the rest of the pellets. Pretend you're singing your favourite 1980s power ballad in a cloud of smoke.

KEY TO SYMBOLS

Every recipe in the book comes with little icons to tell you such important information as whether or not it's suitable for certain diets, how much ice cream the recipe makes and how many people it serves. This is what they look like.

NO CHURN   NON DAIRY   VEGAN   MAKES 1 L   MAKES PIECES   MAKES SAUCE   MAKES POPS   SERVES

CREAMY

DENSE CHOCOLATE BROWNIES WITH VANILLA ICE CREAM

"I don't do vanilla." "Sorry, no, I don't do vanilla." "No! I don't do vanilla!" You're still asking? Okay, I'll do vanilla. Just this once. But only if it's sandwiched between two dense, dark slabs of chocolate brownie. Really filling, really deep, really luxurious.

This brownie is based on a recipe from my friend Cathy. She is the proud owner of a lovely pink and white VW camper van called Lulabelle, from which she serves coffee and cakes. I've embellished the recipe with some cocoa nibs (available from some wholefood shops) and a pinch of coffee.

VANILLA ICE CREAM

1 vanilla pod
350 ml / 12 fl oz / 1½ cups double cream
350 ml / 12 fl oz / 1½ cups whole milk
140 g / 5 oz / generous ½ cup sugar
6 large egg yolks
a pinch of salt, or to taste

MAKES

1+ L

VANILLA ICE CREAM

1. Split the vanilla pod lengthways with a knife and scrape out the seeds. Place the seeds and pod in a saucepan with the cream and milk. Bring it all to a simmer, then remove from the heat and let the flavour infuse for 10 minutes.

2. Whisk the sugar and egg yolks in a large bowl until pale and thick. Pour or ladle the warmed cream slowly into the yolks. Stir with each addition until the custard is blended.

3. As long as the pan hasn't been scorched as a result of step 1, transfer the custard back into it. (If the cream has caught on the bottom, use a clean pan.)

4. On the gentlest heat your hob can muster, warm the custard, stirring slowly for 10–15 minutes. Your aim is to lightly cook the egg and thicken the custard. Use too much heat and the egg will scramble; too much vigorous stirring and not enough heat will get through. Be gentle.

5. Test the custard is ready by checking it on the back of your spoon or spatula. The custard is ready when you notice a change in consistency on the back of your spoon. Taste it, and add salt to your liking.

6. Let your custard cool right down and refrigerate it for at least 4 hours. When it's thoroughly chilled, churn in a machine, or stir-freeze: put the tub in your freezer, then every 30 minutes bring it out and mash the frozen edges with a fork, or use a hand blender to break up the ice crystals. You'll need to do this 3 or 4 times, until smooth and firm.

I use egg yolks to thicken the custard for the pale yellow colour. It's just as good to make a paste with 1½ tbsp cornflour if you don't want the leftover egg whites. For a texture so smooth it's almost shiny and chewy, omit the double cream, and whisk the cooling custard into 250 g / 9 oz / 1 cup mascarpone.

DENSE CHOCOLATE BROWNIES CONTINUED

MAKES
12–14
BROWNIES

BROWNIES

350 g/12 oz 70 % cocoa-solids chocolate, grated or chopped

250 g/9 oz unsalted butter, cubed

1 tsp instant coffee granules

3 large eggs

250 g/9 oz/1 generous cup caster sugar

80 g/3 oz/generous ½ cup plain flour

2 tsp baking powder

6 tsp cocoa powder

a pinch of salt

55 g/2 oz/generous ⅓ cup cocoa nibs (or high cocoa-solids chocolate, chopped)

1 quantity vanilla ice cream (page 16)

BROWNIES

1. Preheat the oven to 160°C/325°F/Gas mark 3. Line two cake tins measuring 18 cm/7 in square with baking parchment; silicone baking moulds the same size will do too.

2. Melt the chocolate and the butter together: place the chocolate in a bowl set over a pan of barely simmering water, making sure hot water does not touch the base of the bowl. Add the diced butter and stir. When the mix is completely liquid, stir in the coffee granules and set aside.

3. In a large bowl, whisk the eggs well, then add the sugar and continue whisking for a few minutes. Fold the chocolate mixture into the eggs.

4. Sift the dry ingredients over the bowl. Fold gently into the chocolate and egg mixture, sprinkle on the cocoa nibs and fold them in too.

5. Divide the brownie batter between the two tins and bake in the oven for 20–25 minutes. To test if the brownies are ready, prick them with a knife – it should come out sticky, but not wet. Allow the slabs to cool on a wire rack then pop them into the freezer.

6. Leave the vanilla ice cream at room temperature for about 20 minutes to soften before you are ready to assemble the cake. (You can also use it straight from churning.) Lay your frozen chocolate slabs on a tray – they'll be nice and cold, so won't melt the ice cream. Spread the vanilla ice cream evenly over one brownie cake and sandwich the second on top.

7. Freeze the brownie sandwich for two hours. When it's firmed up, chop it into whatever shapes you like. My favourite is to slice the brownie into long finger shapes, as they melt so nicely on the tongue. Before serving, leave at room temperature for about 30 minutes.

If your tin is larger than stated here, your mixture will spread more thinly and so cook quicker – reduce the cooking time by 10 minutes and test the brownie by dipping a sharp knife into the centre to see if it comes out sticky. If you have a smaller tin, keep back some mixture, or reduce the cooking time.

VERY STRAWBERRY

This is an eggless, no-churn recipe bursting with fruit. In my work as a food stylist, I often have to pick through boxes of strawberries trying to find the 'perfect' one. So when you see an advert featuring a plump, heart-shaped, not too big, not too small strawberry, complete with a spotless green frill, think of the food stylist assigning hundreds of lesser specimens to the reject pile, denting their confidence for life. All strawberries are beautiful, if you ask me.

350 g/12 oz strawberries
170 g/6 oz/scant ¾ cup sugar
juice of 1 small lemon
300 ml/10 fl oz/1¼ cups double cream, chilled
70 g/2½ oz/scant ½ cup icing sugar
170 g/6 oz full-fat Greek yogurt

NO CHURN   MAKES

1 L

1. Hull and chop the strawberries. Mix with the sugar and half the lemon juice in a pan, put a lid on and set on a very low heat for 4–5 minutes. Keep an eye on the mixture in case it bubbles up, which you should avoid. When you lift the lid, the fruit will have shrunk into its juices. Pour this strawberry compote into a bowl and set aside to cool.

2. When the mix is cold, pulse it with a hand blender and chill until ready to use.

3. To make the ice cream, combine the cream, icing sugar, remaining lemon juice and half the chilled strawberry compote in a large bowl. Whisk until the mixture produces soft peaks, about 5–8 minutes, or sooner with an electric whisk. Fold the rest of the strawberry mixture into the yogurt, then fold this into the strawberry cream.

4. Scoop it all into a lovely pink pillow and put in a tub to freeze overnight. Before serving, soften in the fridge for 10 minutes.

I prefer this eggless, no-churn method for any fruit that's tangy. I find that a custard base dulls the slight sharpness of the berries.

CHOCOLATE

This chocolate ice cream has a rich taste and a super-smooth texture.

If you want to jazz it up, freestyle with a pinch of spice added to the sugar at the start – cinnamon, ginger, or chilli flakes are great.

2 tbsp cocoa powder
180 g/6¼ oz/¾ cup sugar
a pinch of spice, to taste (optional)
425 ml/15 fl oz/scant 2 cups
    double cream
a pinch of salt
75 g/2½ oz 70 % cocoa-solids chocolate,
    grated or finely chopped

MAKES
1 L

1. Mix the cocoa powder with the sugar and any spices you are using. Pop the mix into a saucepan with 250 ml/9 fl oz/1 cup of water and bring to a simmer. Cook the cocoa as if you were making hot chocolate, stirring it on a low heat for 5–6 minutes until the ingredients are blended and the sugar has dissolved.

2. Add the cream and a pinch of salt and warm the cocoa mixture through on the hob. Then add the chocolate, take the pan off the hob and leave the chocolate to melt for a few minutes. Whisk the chocolate cream until it is glossy. Let it cool. To speed up the process, you can place the chocolate cream in a bowl, put this in a larger bowl of iced water and whisk.

3. When the mix is cool, put it to chill in the fridge. Once completely cold, churn in a machine or stir-freeze: put the tub in your freezer, then every 30 minutes bring it out and mash the frozen edges with a fork, or use a hand blender to break up the ice crystals. You'll need to do this 3 or 4 times, until smooth and firm.

4. Before serving, soften in the fridge for 20 minutes.

TASTE PYRAMID

This pyramid represents the popularity of
ice cream types as manufacturers see it.
Vanilla dominates the market, followed by
strawberry and chocolate. Ginger's range sits
underneath all this, with ingredients you
might not have had in an ice cream before.
Cream, milk, sugar and eggs are the
perfect blank canvas to experiment
with flavours. If you've had a
flavour combination that works
in any other kind of dish,
why not try it out in
a basic custard mix
for yourself?

MOCHA CHOCOLATTE–YA–YA!

There was a time when splitting the vanilla pod to release the seeds became fashionable in cookery; before that the little black flecks were deemed dirty-looking. I bring this up only because most recipes using ground coffee would put it in as liquid espresso. The coffee I use is ground really fine; it's powdery, so much of it will pass through mesh. If you can't grind it so fine, substitute a tablespoon of instant espresso granules.

Oh, and don't eat this before bed. It's caffeine-loaded and richer than a banker who's just won the Lottery!

ESPRESSO ICE CREAM

500 ml/18 fl oz/2 cups double cream
250 ml/9 fl oz/1 cup whole milk
2 tbsp finely ground espresso beans
2–3 tbsp coffee syrup
5 large egg yolks
½ tsp vanilla extract
80 g/3 oz/⅓ cup sugar

CHOCOLATE SAUCE

210 ml/7½ fl oz/scant 1 cup freshly
   boiled water from a kettle
55 g/2 oz/scant ⅓ cup cocoa
120 g/4¼ oz/½ cup sugar
100 g/3½ oz 70 % cocoa-solids chocolate,
   grated or finely chopped

MAKES 1 L

MAKES 0.5 L SAUCE

ESPRESSO ICE CREAM

1. Bring the cream, milk, coffee and coffee syrup to a simmer in a saucepan. Turn off the heat and allow the flavours to infuse for a few minutes. In a bowl, mix the egg yolks, vanilla extract and sugar thoroughly.

2. Use a fine sieve to strain the cream into the egg mixture, filtering out most of the coffee grounds. To prevent the eggs in the mix cooking, pour just a third of the cream through at a time, mixing as you go.

3. Put the custard back in the pan over a low heat and stir slowly until it thickens. It is ready when you notice a change in consistency on the back of a spoon. Remove from the heat.

4. Let the custard cool completely, then churn in a machine, or stir-freeze: put the tub in your freezer, then every 30 minutes mash the frozen edges with a fork, until smooth and firm.

CHOCOLATE SAUCE

1. Make this on the day you want to serve the ice cream. Stir the hot water into the cocoa and sugar in a saucepan and bring to a simmer. Stir slowly on a gentle heat for about 5 minutes, to cook out the raw flavour from the cocoa. Turn off the heat. Add the chocolate and allow it to melt, giving it a good stir.

2. To serve, scoop a generous amount of ice cream into a bowl and top with the warm sauce.

To decorate this with white coffee beans, melt 50 g/1¾ oz white chocolate, then drown a couple of tablespoons of whole coffee beans in it. Dredge them out with a fork onto greaseproof paper and allow to set.

COOL CHERRY CREAM

A bit of a wild card comes to the world of ice cream – goat's cheese. I use a soft, mild and very fresh-tasting Welsh goat's cheese. It gives a lovely balance with the tart cherries in the sweet custard base.

I buy either frozen cherries or ones that come in a jar. Fresh ones are too fiddly to stone. As an alternative to cherries, 100g/3½ oz lemon curd works brilliantly.

1 tbsp cornflour

350 ml/12 fl oz/1½ cups whole milk

150 ml/5 fl oz/scant ⅔ cup double cream

160 g/5½ oz/⅔ cup sugar

160 g/5½ oz/1 cup cherries, chopped

200 g/7 oz/scant 1 cup soft goat's cheese

MAKES

1 L

1. Make the cornflour into a paste with a little liquid. If the cherries are quite wet, give them a gentle squeeze over a fine sieve, and use the juice to mix with the cornflour. Alternatively, use a little of the milk. You need to make 3 tbsp of smooth paste.

2. In a saucepan, bring the rest of the milk and the cream to a simmer with the sugar. Add the chopped cherries to the pan. Pour the cornflour paste slowly into the warm liquid, stirring all the time to prevent lumps. Continue to stir until you have a thickened pink custard.

3. Mash the goat's cheese in a bowl. The best way to incorporate the custard is to add it a little at a time, working it in with a fork. Let the mixture go completely cold before chilling it in the fridge for at least 4 hours; this allows the flavours to infuse.

4. Churn it in a machine, or stir-freeze: put the tub in your freezer, then every 30 minutes bring it out and mash the frozen edges with a fork, or use a hand blender to break up the ice crystals. You'll need to do this 3 or 4 times, until smooth and firm.

5. Before serving, soften in the fridge for 20 minutes.

GINGER EGG CANDY

Particularly sweet, offset with a fiery ginger kick, this is one of the creamiest ice creams ever and is a hit with kids. It's very easy to make, but not especially quick. I won't lie to you – it takes 25 minutes of whisking on my gas hob to thicken the egg-yolk syrup. But, your upper arms get a workout and it gives you time to ponder the big questions in life … like, what's for tea? Or string theory. Or what to do with the egg whites …

160 g/5½ oz/⅔ cup sugar
160 ml/5¼ fl oz/scant ⅔ cup freshly boiled water from a kettle
2.5 cm/1 in root ginger, very finely grated
12 large egg yolks
1 heaped tsp cornflour

NON DAIRY   MAKES   1 L

1. In a jug, dissolve the sugar in the boiled water and add the grated ginger (using a fine hand-held grater, such as a Microplane, to grate the ginger is best).

2. Put the egg yolks in a large heatproof bowl and whisk in the cornflour. Rest the bowl over a saucepan of barely simmering water, making sure that the bottom of the bowl does not touch the water.

3. Start to whisk slowly and after about 5 minutes the heat will come through to start cooking the egg. Add a little of the ginger syrup and whisk more briskly, to stop the mixture catching on the bottom of the bowl. Add the syrup a little at a time as the mixture starts to thicken. Keep adding until you've used up all the syrup. You'll know the mixture is thick enough when you can lift out the whisk and leave a trail across the surface, like thick custard. The mixture will also start to stick to the bottom of the bowl. Remove from the heat and leave to cool.

4. Once cold, spoon the mixture into a tub and freeze for at least 4 hours. You should be able to scoop it straight from the freezer, or after only a few minutes at room temperature.

WHITE CHOCOLATE AND PINK PEPPERCORN

This scoop is lighter than the average chocolate ice cream, as it simply uses milk and white chocolate.

The recipe is infinitely versatile – I often use lemongrass instead of pink peppercorns. Cardamom, bay leaf or anything that's knocking about your spice rack can also pair well with white chocolate.

540 ml/19 fl oz/2⅓ cups whole milk

6 tbsp pink peppercorns, crushed

250 g/9 oz white chocolate, chopped or grated

MAKES

1 L

1. Bring the milk and crushed peppercorns to a simmer in a small saucepan. Turn off the heat and let the mixture infuse for 15 minutes.

2. Strain the liquid to get rid of the peppercorns and return it to the pan to warm to around body temperature. Remove from the heat and add the chocolate. Leave it for a couple of minutes for the chocolate to begin melting, then whisk the mix gently until smooth.

3. Easy! The only catch to this recipe is cooling the mixture. If you leave it alone, you may end up with the chocolate separating and floating above the milk. The trick here is to cool the mix rapidly, so pour it into a bowl placed in a larger bowl of iced water, then stir it until completely cold.

4. Chill in the fridge for at least 4 hours, then churn in a machine, or stir-freeze: put the tub in your freezer, then every 30 minutes bring it out and mash the frozen edges with a fork, or use a hand blender to break up the ice crystals. You'll need to do this 3 or 4 times, until smooth and firm.

5. Before serving, soften in the fridge for 15 minutes.

Great on its own, decorated with a dusting of pink pepper; or serve with a slice of bitter chocolate tart.

GINGER MARBLE MALT ICE CREAM

During a recent summer, I was asked to come up with a flavour to represent Manchester at the UK's Food & Drink Festival. I chose malt grain from the local Marble Beerhouse brewery.

When I came to Manchester 15 years ago, the Ginger Marble pint became a staple fixture in my life. More so than other local delicacies like Vimto, blood pudding or the Manchester tart. Since then, I've experimented with grain from other breweries. The Governor pint was promoted by Marco Pierre White (for JW Lees) and Build a Rocket Boys! was conceived by the band Elbow (for Robinson's). Each has its own subtle characteristics, but the flavour you get is deeply malty and wholesome, like a supercharged Horlicks. Malt powder can be found in wholefood shops; you may need to source the grain from a local brewery.

200 g/7 oz/1½ cups crushed malt grain, or 100 g/3½ oz/¾ cup malt powder
550 ml/19 fl oz/scant 2½ cups whole milk
450 ml/16 fl oz/scant 2 cups double cream
120 g/4¼ oz/½ cup sugar
1 tsp ground ginger
a pinch of hops (optional)
a pinch of salt

MAKES

1 L

1. If you're lucky enough to get hold of real malt grain, you will need to crush it. A good food processor on high speed will do the trick.

2. Bring the milk and cream to boiling point in a saucepan with the grain, sugar, ground ginger and hops, if you are using them. If you have bought malt powder instead of whole grain, mix some of the milk into it to make a thin paste first, to stop it sticking in a solid lump in the pan. Then just mix the paste straight into the rest of the milk.

3. Let your malty milk cook and thicken for 10 minutes on a low heat, stirring it from time to time to stop it catching. The starches in the grain will gradually thicken the mixture. The custard is ready when you notice a change in consistency on the back of your spoon.

4. Strain the liquid through a fine sieve. If you've used grain, balance the sieve over a sturdy bowl, as the grain will fill it. Sieve in stages, pressing the grain to extract as much liquid as possible.

5. Add a pinch of salt and taste. Is it punchy? If not, add a tiny bit more salt and taste again.

6. When the mixture is cool, chill it in the fridge. Then churn in a machine, or stir-freeze: put the tub in your freezer, then every 30 minutes bring it out and mash the frozen edges with a fork, or use a hand blender to break up the ice crystals. You'll need to do this 3 or 4 times, until smooth and firm. Before serving, soften in the fridge for 10–15 minutes.

HONEY AND HALVA SAVARIN

Halva is a type of sweet made from sesame paste. It has a strange texture that resembles unset concrete; and while being very sweet, it has a sharp savoury note. I think it's a flavour that we learn to love with age – a bit like grapefruit or black coffee.

This ice cream sets in a savarin mould or Kugelhopf cake tin; but anything that dips in the middle works. It makes a really attractive and unusual dessert on the table, overflowing with fresh figs, grapes, even cheese – Roquefort is especially good.

5 large eggs

160 g/5½ oz/generous ½ cup strong, dark honey

seeds from 4 cardamom pods, crushed

a pinch of salt

450 ml/16 fl oz/scant 2 cups double cream

150 g/5½ oz/1 cup chopped halva (roughly 1 cm/½ in pieces)

MAKES

1.5 L

1. You will need a 1.5 litre/52 fl oz silicone mould. If you are using a traditional tin of the same size, line it with 2–3 layers of cling film, which will make removing the ice cream easier.

2. Whisk the eggs, honey, crushed cardamom seeds and salt in a heatproof glass bowl until fully blended. Set the bowl over a small amount of simmering water in a pan. Slowly stir the mixture over a low heat. Whisk until it thickens, about 10–15 minutes. When the mixture is thick enough to hold a little ribbony trail on the surface when you lift the whisk, remove from the heat and leave it to cool a little.

3. Whip the cream until the beaters leave a trail. Be careful not to let it get too stiff – softness makes it easier to incorporate the egg mixture without lumps. Fold the egg mixture into the cream with a spatula. If the mixture has separated as it cools, give it a good whisk before adding it to the cream. Fold the little pieces of chopped halva through the cream and egg mixture.

4. Transfer to the mould and freeze for at least 4 hours. To serve, turn out the ice cream and leave for a few minutes before scooping.

Want to see how delicious this looks? See the picture on the preceding page.

CAMEL'S MILK ICE CREAM

"Claire, for this year's Experimental Food Society Spectacular I want you to do something that's never been done before!" said Alexa, the society's founder. Using camel's milk would have been worth doing for the experimentation, fun, and frivolity. But when we looked into it, there were so many health reasons for giving it a go. Raw camel's milk provides all-round nutrition, particularly vitamins B and C; it's low-fat and contains ten times the iron of cow's milk.

Camel's milk itself tastes lovely. It is creamy despite being low in fat – you can almost taste the minerals. Maybe that's why people think it's slightly salty.

Arabic and Somali communities have known about the medicinal properties of camel's milk for millennia. I started getting emails from people wanting the milk to help treat diabetes and Crohn's disease – camel's milk has been linked to improvement in these conditions. I wondered if it could catch on – everyone seemed to enjoy it and the nicest part was knowing that the milk has come from happy animals. Notoriously grumpy, would you want to milk an unhappy camel?

160 g/5½ oz/scant 1 cup icing sugar

500 ml/18 fl oz/2 cups camel's milk

1 tsp rose water (optional)

a squeeze of lemon juice or a drop of vanilla or almond extract, to taste (optional)

1 tsp xanthan gum powder

MAKES
1 L

1. Whisk the icing sugar into the milk in a bowl. Stir in the flavouring if you wish – rose water and lemon juice work well, or add a drop of vanilla or almond extract.

2. Lightly dust the xanthan gum over the milk and use a hand blender to incorporate it. The trick is to skim the surface with the blender, working it down into the milk. (If you dive straight in, the powder can quickly go gummy and cling to the hand blender.) After 30 seconds, you'll notice the milk has thickened.

3. Churn the thickened milk in a machine, or stir-freeze: put the tub in your freezer, then every 30 minutes bring it out and mash the frozen edges with a fork, or use a hand blender to break up the ice crystals. You'll need to do this 3 or 4 times, until smooth and firm. Because of the low fat content in the milk, this ice cream will taste more like a sorbet. Enjoy it for what it is, or introduce more air and smaller ice crystals by going back in with a hand blender before it completely hardens.

You can find camel's milk in Middle Eastern grocer's; xanthan gum is sold in most supermarkets (I use it to thicken the camel's milk before churning because heating the raw milk to make a custard would destroy many of the nutrients). For the same pure-milk flavour, you can use unpasteurised cow's cream if you prefer.

XV OLIVE OIL ICE CREAM WITH SMOKED SEA SALT CRYSTALS

Salt shouldn't be such a surprise ingredient in sweet things. Since various health authorities have made us worry about our salt levels, have you noticed how your favourite biscuits don't taste quite as good?

This ice cream should never taste salty, but adding salt really helps bring out the flavour of the olive oil. I've got a very salty palate and high tolerance for salt. I even like to add extra crystals on top of my scoops.

Salt heightens a flavour but we all use different amounts. Like someone who goes to loads of gigs all the time and gets acclimatised to high volume, we all listen to the same music and taste the same food, but need it amplified to differing degrees. So taste as you go.

If you have only regular sea salt, no matter, but use only the best extra virgin olive oil for this recipe. I'm into Hellenic oil at the moment, as it's so peppery and grassy.

200 ml/7 fl oz/scant 1 cup whole milk
100 ml/3½ fl oz/scant ½ cup double cream
140 g/5 oz/generous ½ cup sugar
5 large egg yolks
160 ml/5¼ fl oz/⅔ cup extra virgin olive oil
a pinch of Maldon smoked sea salt, or your choice of smoked sea salt, plus extra for serving

MAKES

0.75 L

1. Bring the milk, cream and sugar to the boil in a saucepan, stirring to dissolve the sugar. Remove from the heat and set aside.

2. Beat the egg yolks until pale and thick. Slowly add the milk and cream mixture to the yolks, stirring as you go. Transfer the mixture back to the pan and keep stirring slowly over a gentle heat for 5–10 minutes, until it thickens into a custard. It's ready when you notice a change in consistency on the back of your spoon. Leave it to cool.

3. Use a balloon whisk to blend the olive oil and the smoked sea salt into the custard, tasting as you go. The amount of salt you add should be just enough to lift the flavour of the olive oil, which should sharpen noticeably.

4. Let the mixture go completely cold. If it has separated when you come to churn, just give it a good whisk first. For best results, I recommend churning in a machine (stir-freezing may cause the ingredients to separate).

5. Allow 20 minutes for the ice cream to soften in the fridge before serving, then serve with an extra pinch of smoked sea salt on top.

If you don't want to end up with lots of leftover egg whites, you can get cartons of pasteurised egg yolk (and whites) from wholesalers. Most will let you make a cash purchase. Ring around the fruit and veg wholesalers in your area. These are the guys who will usually stock them.

CLOTTED ICED CREAM AND PEPPERED STRAWBERRY SOUP

This summery dessert started life as a sorbet mix – I just loved the soup as it was when I blended it all up, so I didn't bother to churn it.

Hot and cold things together are just so gorgeous. As invigorating as a kiss and a slap, smooth and dense ice cream melts into warm peppery fruit.

MAKES

1 L

CLOTTED ICED CREAM

125 g/4½ oz/½ cup sugar

grated zest of 1 unwaxed lemon

400 g/14 oz clotted cream

½ tsp vanilla extract

PEPPERED STRAWBERRY SOUP

400 g/14 oz halved strawberries

60 g/2¼ oz/¼ cup sugar

a sprig of fresh mint

½ tsp crushed black peppercorns

zest of ½ an unwaxed lemon

a pinch of salt

CLOTTED ICED CREAM

1. In a small pan, stir together the sugar, lemon zest and 125 ml/4 fl oz/½ cup of water and bring to a simmer. Cook for 2 minutes, then remove from the heat, pour into a bowl and leave to cool.

2. If the clotted cream has a thin, buttery crust on top, scrape it off. Then, whisk the cream into the cooled syrup. Add the vanilla extract.

3. Churn in a machine, or stir-freeze: put the tub in your freezer, then every 30 minutes mash the frozen edges with a fork, until smooth and firm.

PEPPERED STRAWBERRY SOUP

1. To make the soup, combine all the ingredients in a pan with 4 tbsp of water, letting all the sugar coat the fruit. Put a lid on the pan and leave on a medium–low heat for 5–10 minutes. Keep an eye on it to make sure it doesn't bubble up. When you see the strawberries swimming in lots of lovely red poaching liquor, turn off the heat and let them sit for 10 minutes.

2. Remove the sprig of mint and blend the strawberries well, using a hand blender. Strain the soup through a fine sieve and let it cool. This will keep in the fridge for up to 5 days if you're not eating it straightaway.

3. To serve, let the ice cream soften in the fridge for 20 minutes and keep the soup at room temperature. Serve a generous scoop with a little soup poured over the top.

GORGONZOLA AND HONEY

I wasn't sure if such an unlikely-sounding ice cream would sell from the van, but on one lovely summer's day it really did.

I let people sample things first and there's always a tense few seconds before they deliver their verdict. Predictably, this isn't the ice cream for everyone. But enough people, including children – shock! – loved it. Pale pistachio in colour, it's sweet with a subtle, zingy blue-cheese back note.

250 ml/9 fl oz/1 cup whole milk
250 ml/9 fl oz/1 cup double cream
4 large egg yolks
160 g/5½ oz/⅔ cup honey
55g/2 oz Gorgonzola cheese, crumbled

MAKES

1 L

1. Heat the milk and cream in a saucepan to just below boiling point.

2. In a bowl, lightly whisk the yolks with 3 tbsp of the honey until the egg is well combined.

3. Ladle some of the warmed cream and milk into the honey mixture and stir well. Continue until all the cream is incorporated, then pour this back into the pan (as long as the bottom of the pan is not scorched). Over a low heat, slowly keep the mixture moving with a wooden spoon until it thickens. The custard is ready when you notice a change in consistency on the back of your spoon.

4. Now stir in the remaining honey and the Gorgonzola. Whisk to make sure all the cheese is melted in. Cool the custard as quickly as you can. A good method is to transfer it to a bowl, and plunge the base into a larger bowl of iced water, giving it a good stir.

5. When the custard is cool, chill it in the fridge. Once completely cold, churn it in a machine, or stir-freeze: put the tub in your freezer, then every 30 minutes bring it out and mash the frozen edges with a fork, or use a hand blender to break up the ice crystals. You'll need to do this 3 or 4 times, until smooth and firm.

6. To serve, let the ice cream soften in the fridge for 10–15 minutes before scooping.

FRUITY

EASY BERRY RIPPLE

This meringue-based ice cream is more like a frozen fool. The choice of fruit is entirely down to you. A can of ready-made fruit pie filling or a good-quality jar of compote will work fine (or try making your own – see note below). Don't use jam, though, as the sugar content can be too high.

2 large egg whites
110 g/3½ oz/scant ½ cup icing sugar, sifted
350 ml/12 fl oz/1½ cups double cream
450 g/1 lb good-quality fruit compote

NO CHURN

MAKES

1 L

1. First make a meringue by whisking the egg whites. You need a very clean bowl, and the whites should be free from any traces of yolk. Whisk until soft peaks begin to form.

2. Now add about a third of the sifted icing sugar. Continue to whisk until the meringue mixture feels thick. Repeat with the rest of the sugar. Keep whisking until it stands in soft peaks.

3. In another bowl, whip the cream to the same consistency, until soft peaks form.

4. Fold together the cream and meringue. Make sure the two are well incorporated but be careful not to knock out too much air.

5. Swirl in the fruit. This is best done by covering the surface of the ice-cream mixture with a good layer of compote before going back in with the spatula in a folding motion. Stop folding while there are still thick, glossy streaks of fruit against the white cream. Gently scoop into a tub and leave to freeze overnight.

6. Give the berry ripple 5 minutes to soften a little in the fridge before serving.

Making your own compote is straightforward. Simply simmer your fruit with half its weight in sugar and a little lemon juice until syrupy. Some fruit will give a more watery result than others, but will still work. As well as berries, apricots, plums and other fibrous fruits are ideal.

DURIAN CHOC ICE

When you mention durian to people who have travelled across Southeast Asia, they'll reminisce about signs on public transport banning the fruit, owing to its stench. Well I adore the smell of perfectly ripened durian – floral, musky and exotic. And it has the custardy, soft texture of avocado, so it's win-win. I also love its piercing skin, which has thorns like a rose.

You can buy fresh durian from Chinese supermarkets, or frozen if it's out of season. A thick wedge is enough. I recommend keeping the fruit in an airtight container and storing it somewhere well ventilated … such as your garden (right down at the bottom …).

DURIAN ICE CREAM

170 g/6 oz/¾ cup durian flesh (no pith or stone)
250 ml/9 fl oz/1 cup whole milk
250 ml/9 fl oz/1 cup double cream
4 large egg yolks
3 tbsp sugar
a pinch of salt

CHOC ICE

250 g/9 oz dark chocolate

MAKES 0.75 L

MAKES 10–12 CHOC ICES

DURIAN ICE CREAM

1. Make a smooth paste from the durian by mashing it well with a fork, or blend for 1 minute with a hand blender.

2. Put the milk and cream in a saucepan and bring to a simmer over a medium heat. Cook for 3–4 minutes while you whisk the egg yolks with the sugar and salt. Either ladle the milk and cream slowly into the egg and sugar, or transfer it to a jug and pour it in gradually. Whisk the cream and egg mixture together.

3. Pour the mixture into a clean pan. On a gentle heat, begin to cook the custard, being very careful not to scramble it. The custard is ready when you notice a change in consistency on the back of your spoon. Remove the pan from the heat.

4. Add the durian paste and whisk energetically for 1 minute to cool.

5. Let the custard cool to room temperature, giving it a good whisk every now and again, then chill it thoroughly in the fridge.

6. Churn in a machine, or stir-freeze: put the tub in your freezer, then every 30 minutes bring it out and mash the frozen edges with a fork, or use a hand blender to break up the ice crystals. You'll need to do this 3 or 4 times, until smooth and firm.

CHOC ICE

1. Line a flat tray or plate with baking parchment. Break up the dark chocolate, place the pieces in a heatproof bowl and melt over a pan of barely simmering water. Remove from the heat.

2. Retrieve the ice cream (if stir-freezing, do this before the ice cream sets too hard). Spread it into a square silicone cake mould, freeze until completely firm, then cut into 10–12 small bricks. Or scoop the set ice cream into balls and push a lolly stick into each ball.

3. Dip the bricks or balls into the melted chocolate then pop them onto the lined tray or plate. Refreeze for at least 30 minutes.

TUTTI FRUTTI FIREBALL

Tutti frutti – an ice-cream flavour literally meaning "all fruits", yet tasting of none in particular. This is Baked Alaska, flambéed! Well, when you get to a certain age only so many candles will fit on a cake, so why not set the whole thing on fire?

When I made a Tutti Frutti Fireball for the first time at a birthday cocktail party, everyone craned their necks to watch it go up. It works brilliantly. A mound of ice-cream cake covered in snowy, burning meringue is visually stunning – and you look pretty hard doing it! Make the ice cream a day before you need to serve it.

TUTTI FRUTTI ICE CREAM

100 g/3½ oz/1 cup pistachios, chopped
250 g/9 oz/1½ cups glacé cherries, roughly chopped
10 dried apricots, roughly chopped
100 g/3½ oz/½ cup mixed candied peel
180 g/6¼ oz/generous 1 cup icing sugar
3 tbsp lemon juice
4 tbsp peach schnapps, or any fruity liqueur you have to hand
600 ml/35 fl oz/2½ cups double cream

THE FIREBALL

1 panettone
6 large egg whites
350 g/12 oz/scant 1½ cups caster sugar
200 ml/7 fl oz/scant 1 cup rum, or any spirit with 40 % alcohol content

SERVES
10–12

TUTTI FRUTTI ICE CREAM

1. You will need a 1.5 litre/52 fl oz pudding basin in which to freeze the ice cream and a lipped oven tray to hold the fiery rum that spills off when you flambé it.

2. Combine the chopped pistachios, cherries, apricots and mixed peel in a bowl and set aside. Sift the icing sugar into a large bowl and blend in the lemon juice and peach schnapps. Chill this mixture in the fridge for 10 minutes.

3. Once the sugar and liqueur mix is cold, add the cream and whisk until it forms soft peaks. Fold in the fruit and nuts and scoop it all into the pudding basin. Freeze overnight.

THE FIREBALL

1. About 30–60 minutes before you want to serve the Fireball, preheat your oven to its highest setting. Get the ice cream out of the freezer, keeping it in its basin.

2. To make the base of the Baked Alaska, cut a slice 5 cm/2 in thick from the bottom of the panettone and fit it over the top of the pudding basin. Press the panettone down to stick it to the ice cream and fill in any gaps with more slices from the loaf. Make sure no ice cream is poking through. Pop the basin back into the freezer while you make the meringue.

3. In a large, clean bowl, whisk the egg whites to firm peaks. Add the caster sugar in four stages, whisking well between each addition. Keep whisking until the meringue is thick and glossy.

4. When the oven has reached its highest temperature, it's time to extract the ice cream. Ease it away from the pudding basin by submerging the bowl in hot water for about 20 seconds. Sit the ice cream on the lipped oven tray. Smother with the meringue, making pretty peaks and swirls. Make sure the meringue covers all the ice cream and the panettone, then bake in the oven for 4–5 minutes or until lightly browned all over.

5. In the meantime, warm the rum in a small saucepan over a low heat until it begins to bubble – don't let it boil. The heat will help it to catch light and stay alight for longer.

6. Gather your guests. Take the pan off the heat, then ignite the rum with a long match. Douse the pudding with the fiery booze, using a large, long-handled serving spoon. Serve when the flames have burned out.

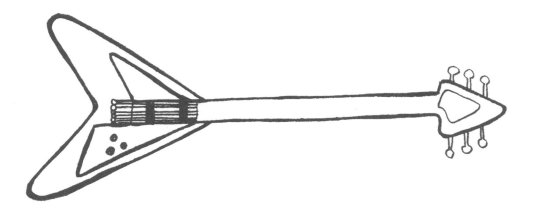

Just to be on the safe side, I keep a damp tea towel nearby in case anything other than the Fireball catches light. However, as long as you keep the area that you're working in clear, and put the pudding in a tin with a decent lip to catch the hot rum, this pudding for pyros should be completely safe.

COCONUT AND ROAST BANANA WITH TAMARIND RIPPLE

This doesn't feel like a vegan ice cream, although it is, as it's so naturally creamy.

Whenever I make anything vegan, I'm reminded of TV presenters the Two Fat Ladies, with their hilariously thin grasp of animal-free diets: "... This is most suitable for vegetarians, there's hardly any meat in it at all."

4 large bananas
70 g/2½ oz/scant ⅓ cup sugar
a pinch of salt
400 ml/14 fl oz/1¾ cups unsweetened, full-fat coconut milk
1 tbsp tamarind paste
1 tsp icing sugar
fresh coconut shavings and lime zest, to serve

VEGAN   MAKES   1 L

1. Set the oven to 180°C/350°F/Gas mark 4. Roast the bananas in their skins for about 15 minutes until blackened and soft.

2. While the bananas are still warm, slide the flesh out of the skins and mash it with the sugar. Add the pinch of salt and the coconut milk. Using a hand blender, purée the mix until it is completely smooth.

3. Churn in a machine or stir-freeze (see steps 4 and 5). While the ice cream is freezing, in a small bowl add a teaspoon of warm water to the tamarind paste to loosen it and mix in the icing sugar. Set this aside until the ice cream has frozen.

4. If you've churned in a machine, ripple the tamarind through the ice cream when it's finished. Use a fork to draw lines of the tamarind through the ice cream, then fold it all over a couple of times. Tamarind is a strong flavour, so try to do this evenly.

5. If you're stir-freezing, this is a great ice cream to finish in a food processor; you will get the best possible texture. When the ice cream is frozen firm, quickly transfer it to the food processor and pulse for no longer than a minute, until smooth. Scoop it all back into the tub and ripple through the tamarind, as in step 4. Return to the freezer.

6. Allow a good 25 minutes to soften the ice cream in the fridge before serving. To serve, decorate the scoops with shavings of fresh coconut and lime zest.

This is the perfect dessert to serve after tucking into a hot Thai green curry.

CLEMENTINE AND OLIVE OIL

A sweet and zingy sorbet, with a lush, grassy smoothness. As with the XV Olive Oil ice cream (page 36), choose an oil that's good enough to use in a salad.

This recipe is an opportunity to try an unusual ingredient for a home cook – soya lecithin, available at healthfood stores. Just like the lecithin inside an egg yolk binds fat to water, soya lecithin emulsifies. It's not vital, but it gives the sorbet a smoother finish. I recommend using an ice-cream machine, and serving this freshly churned.

350 ml/12 fl oz/1½ cups juice from 10–12 clementines, or 5 mandarins
5 tbsp icing sugar
140 ml/4¾ fl oz/generous ½ cup olive oil
a drop of vanilla extract (optional)
1 tbsp soya lecithin granules (optional)

VEGAN

MAKES

0.5 L

1. Strain the fruit juice through a fine sieve. Mix the juice with the icing sugar and olive oil, and the vanilla extract and soya lecithin, if using. Mix with a hand blender for 2 minutes or until the lecithin granules completely break down.

2. To remove any obstinate bits, strain the mix a second time through a fine sieve.

3. Pop the mix in the coldest part of your fridge for an hour. For the best results, churn it in a machine and serve straightaway. The oil content means that it'll never be as nice to scoop once it's frozen hard. If you do freeze it, give it 30 minutes in the fridge before you dig in.

RASPBERRY AND ROSE PAVLOVA

Imagine meringue that's crisp on the outside and chewy in the middle, coupled with the summery tang of fragrant berries. Notoriously, the strength of rose water brands differs, so taste your ice-cream mix, adding more until the taste comes through. Once you've made the meringue, this recipe is superquick. It's completely delicious either served straight from the freezer or thawed until the cream is soft.

SERVES
10–12

MERINGUE

6 large egg whites
350 g/12 oz/1½ cups caster sugar
1 tsp cornflour

ROSE PETALS

1 rose (pesticide free)
1 large egg white, lightly beaten
3 tbsp caster sugar

ICE CREAM

225 g/8 oz/1 cup raspberries
a squeeze of lemon juice
160 g/5¾ oz/1 cup icing sugar
2 tsp rose water, or to taste
300 ml/10 fl oz/1¼ cups double cream

MERINGUE

1. Preheat the oven to 180°C/350°F/Gas mark 4. Line a flat baking tray with baking parchment or a silicone mat.

2. In a large, scrupulously clean bowl, whisk the egg whites until they become lush and snowy. Add half the sugar and continue whisking for a minute, or until the mixture starts to look glossy. Add the rest of the sugar and the cornflour, and whisk until you have a thick, shiny, viscous meringue. To see if it's ready, a good test is to hold the bowl upside down. Does it hold? If yes, it's done; if not, sorry, you'll want to clean that up.

3. Spoon the meringue into a round pile on the baking tray. As long as the meringue is thick enough, it will behave and won't seep towards the edge. If it's too runny and you face culinary emergency, simply scrape it back in and pour it into a lined 10 in/22 cm cake tin instead.

4. Bake on the middle shelf of the oven for 40 minutes – although keep an eye on it for the last 10 minutes, as oven temperatures vary. Let the meringue cool gradually by turning off the oven but leaving the tray inside it. The oven will also be at the perfect temperature to make the rose decoration.

You could use the egg yolks for another ice-cream recipe; or try this sauce, which you can use as a dip or as a gratin on top of moussaka or pasta. Whisk 6 egg yolks with a pinch of salt and 2 tbsp of water in a bowl and set over a pan of simmering water. When the mixture's creamy, whisk in 50 g/1¾ oz finely grated parmesan cheese.

ROSE PETALS

1. Line a baking tray with baking parchment. Lightly whisk the egg white with a fork, then pick off the best petals from your rose, and dip them into the whites, or smooth egg white over each with your finger. Dust with sugar and lay them on the baking tray. Put the tray into the oven when you have turned it off to cool your meringue, or reset the oven to its lowest temperature to dry the petals for 40 minutes. When they cool down, the petals will crisp.

ICE CREAM

1. Reserve 10 raspberries to decorate the top of the dessert. Mash the rest with a good squeeze of lemon and 110 g/3½ oz/generous ½ cup of the icing sugar.

2. Mix the rose water and remaining icing sugar into the cream. Whip it until it holds its shape but remains soft. Fold in the raspberry mixture. If the mixture produces marbling, rather than a uniform pinkness, that's okay. Taste and add a little more rose water, if necessary.

3. Spread the mixture over the top of your meringue, leaving a good couple of inches of the crust showing at the edges. Top with the reserved raspberries. Freeze the pavlova for at least 2–4 hours.

4. If it's been in the freezer all night, let it thaw for 10 minutes before serving. Dot the rose petals over the top before you bring it to the table.

GINGER SLING WITH A PINEAPPLE HEART

This recipe is a warm, gingery rice pudding with a roasted pineapple sorbet. The pineapple sorbet is quite intense – that's why I've paired it with soothing, milky carbs. I've measured the sorbet to use up a whole pineapple, even though it makes more sorbet than you need. You can always halve the amounts, or freeze leftovers for up to four weeks. The rice pudding can be made in advance, but make sure you cool it rapidly and store it in the fridge. Reheat with a splash more milk on the hob or in a microwave.

SERVES
6

SORBET

1 smallish fresh pineapple, the flesh weighing about 550 g/1 lb 4 oz when chopped
200 g/7 oz/1 cup caster sugar
juice of ½ a lemon

RICE PUDDING

185 g/6½ oz/scant 1 cup Arborio or pudding rice
300 ml/10 fl oz/1¼ cups whole milk
400 ml/14 fl oz/1¾ cups full-fat coconut milk (or whole milk again, if you prefer)
70 g/2½ oz/scant ⅓ cup sugar
3 tbsp finely grated root ginger

SORBET

1. Set your grill to its highest setting. Line a baking tray with aluminium foil. Cut away the outer skin of the pineapple, getting rid of all the little black pits. Slice down and remove all the flesh from the core, then chop into chunks; lay these over the baking tray. Grill for 5–8 minutes, until they start to blacken around the edges. Toss them about to cook evenly.

2. When the pineapple is ready, tip the chunks into a jug or a bowl. Add the sugar and 125 ml/4 fl oz/½ cup of water. Add the lemon juice. Give it a good stir and blitz with a hand blender or a food processor for 3–4 minutes, until completely smooth.

3. Strain this mixture through a fine sieve to remove any fibres. Taste, adding a touch more lemon juice if the mixture is overpoweringly sweet. Leave to cool.

4. Chill the mixture in the fridge, then churn in a machine, or stir-freeze: put the tub in your freezer, then every 30 minutes mash the frozen edges with a fork, until smooth and firm.

RICE PUDDING

1. Combine all the ingredients in a small pan and bring slowly to the boil, stirring. Simmer for 20–25 minutes, until the rice is cooked, stirring from time to time. Let the pudding cool slightly before serving.

2. To serve, divide the pudding between 6 bowls and top with a scoop of the pineapple sorbet. Owing to the high sugar content, the sorbet should be fairly soft straight from the freezer, but it might need 5 minutes at room temperature to scoop well.

The tiny inner leaves from the very top of the pineapple make a cute retro decoration. They come out easily with a little tug.

APPLE FOOL WITH MINCEMEAT GRANITA AND HONEY CRUMBS

A dessert of textures – soft cream, spiced ice and a sweet crunch – this is reminiscent of a stuffed baked apple, and when you take a mouthful it's not immediately obvious which flavours match which textures.

Don't worry if you haven't got all the spices listed for the granita – just use what you do have to make a spicy syrup. If grape molasses is hard to find, use treacle instead.

SERVES

6+

MINCEMEAT GRANITA

85 g/3 oz/⅓ cup sugar

juice and zest of ½ an unwaxed lemon

2 tsp grape molasses

½ tsp each of fennel seeds, ground coriander, cinnamon, ginger and nutmeg

HONEY CRUMBS

1 heaped tbsp set honey or 2 tbsp runny honey

5 heaped tbsp rolled oats

25 g/1 oz butter, softened

2 tbsp sugar

APPLE FOOL

2 large Bramley apples, peeled, cored and cut into chunks

200 g/7 oz/generous ¾ cup sugar

juice of ½ a lemon

300 ml/10 fl oz/1¼ cups whipping cream

80 g/3 oz/½ cup icing sugar

MINCEMEAT GRANITA

1. Put all the ingredients with 160 ml/5¼ fl oz/⅔ cup of water into a saucepan, stir and simmer for 3–4 minutes. Turn off the heat. Add another 125 ml/4 fl oz/½ cup of water and stir.

2. Strain the liquid through a fine sieve and leave to cool. When the syrup is completely cold, pop it into the freezer. Stir every 20 minutes or so to break up the ice and prevent it freezing into a solid block. You should end up with icy crystals.

HONEY CRUMBS

1. Preheat the oven to 180°C/350°F/Gas mark 4. Line a baking tray with baking parchment. Melt the honey in a saucepan. Put the oats in a bowl, stir in the sugar and then rub in the butter with your fingertips.

2. Spread the mixture over the baking sheet, pour the melted honey over the top, and bake for 10 minutes, until golden. Allow to cool, then rub between your fingers to produce fine, crunchy crumbs.

APPLE FOOL

1. Gently stew the apple with the sugar until it's a thick, soft mass. Squeeze in the lemon juice and stir well. It should have a thick purée consistency, with the odd lump. Allow to cool.

2. Mix the cream with the icing sugar, and whip to soft peaks. Fold the cold apple purée into the cream.

3. Before serving, soften the granita in the fridge for 15 minutes. Spoon the apple fool into small glasses. Rough up the granita with a fork and scatter some shards over the fools. To finish, sprinkle a tablespoon of honey crumbs in each glass.

FENNEL AND PEACH

This straightforward, custard-based ice cream is fragrant with fresh peach and mild aniseed notes. I often combine shavings of fennel with blue cheese and peach slices in a salad. I'll never bite into a peach, though. That fuzzy skin is like sucking on velvet – give me a nectarine any day ...

You can use either peaches or nectarines in this recipe as we're skinning the fruit and they work the same way when unrobed.

6 ripe peaches
450 ml/16 fl oz/scant 2 cups whole milk
450 ml/16 fl oz/scant 2 cups double cream
3 heaped tbsp fennel seeds, crushed
6 large egg yolks
170 g/6 oz/scant ¾ cup sugar

MAKES

1.5 L

1. Skin the peaches by putting them in a bowl, pouring boiling water over them and leaving them for 30 seconds, then plunging them into cold water. Peel them – the skin will come away easily – and rip the flesh from the stones. Blend the fruit into a purée using a hand blender or liquidizer. You should have around 450 g/16 oz/scant 2 cups of fruit purée.

2. Bring the milk and cream to simmering point in a saucepan with the crushed fennel seeds. Remove from the heat and let the flavour develop for 10 minutes. In the meantime, beat the egg yolks with the sugar, until pale and creamy.

3. Strain the milk and cream into the egg yolks and sugar and pour into a saucepan. Slowly stir the custard over a low heat until it thickens. The custard is ready when you notice a change in consistency on the back of your spoon.

4. Let the custard cool, then refrigerate. Once it's cold, whisk in the peach purée. Churn in a machine, or stir-freeze: put the tub in your freezer, then every 30 minutes bring it out and mash the frozen edges with a fork, or use a hand blender to break up the ice crystals. You'll need to do this 3 or 4 times, until smooth and firm.

5. Before serving, soften the ice cream in the fridge for 20 minutes.

JOSTABERRY

What do you get if you cross a gooseberry with a blackcurrant? A jostaberry. I'd never heard of this hybrid before my friend Carolyn gave me a bag from her bountiful garden. I don't know how you coax a blackcurrant into conjugation with a prickly gooseberry – and, frankly, I don't care. The result is deliciously out of the ordinary.

If you can't get hold of jostaberries, substitute 100 g/3½ oz each of blackcurrants and gooseberries instead.

200 g/7 oz jostaberries
200 g/7 oz/generous ¾ cup sugar
1 tbsp cornflour
300 ml/10 fl oz/1¼ cups whole milk
300 ml/10 fl oz/1¼ cups double cream
a pinch of salt

MAKES

1 L

1. On a low heat, simmer the berries with a quarter of the sugar for about 5 minutes, or until the fruit has softened and the liquid has slightly reduced. Leave to cool.

2. Mix the cornflour with a little of the milk to make a loose paste. Heat the milk and cream together in a saucepan, allowing it to simmer for a few minutes. Add the remaining sugar and the cornflour paste, stirring all the time to prevent lumps. Continue to simmer and stir over a medium heat. The custard is ready when you notice a change in consistency on the back of your spoon.

3. Stir in the softened fruit and its juices with the salt and leave to cool. To speed up the process, put the custard in a heatproof bowl and place it in a larger bowl of ice-cold water. To release heat and stop a skin forming, stir the ice-cream mix from time to time. When it is cool, refrigerate it.

4. Churn the ice cream in a machine, or stir-freeze: put the tub in your freezer, then every 30 minutes bring it out and mash the frozen edges with a fork, or use a hand blender to break up the ice crystals. You'll need to do this 3 or 4 times, until smooth and firm.

5. Before serving, soften the ice cream in the fridge for 5–10 minutes.

NUTTY

APRICOT AND ALMOND CAKE

This apricot ice cream is served inside an almond sponge – luscious. Frozen cake is so gratifying and easy to make I don't know why you don't see it more often. Use ripe fruit that tear easily from their stones – but don't throw the stones away; use them in Killer Vanilla with Apricot Kernel ice cream (page 74). I've tried infusing the delicate flavour of the stones into the milk for this recipe, but the tangy fruit overpowered them. They needed a dish all of their own.

ALMOND SPONGE

155 g/5½ oz butter, softened
155 g/5½ oz/1 cup icing sugar
3 large eggs
200 g/7 oz/1¾ cup ground almonds

APRICOT ICE CREAM

6 to 8 ripe apricots
200 g/7 oz/generous ¾ cup sugar
seeds from 4 cardamom pods (optional)
300 ml/10 fl oz/1¼ cups whole milk
300 ml/10 fl oz/1¼ cups double cream
5 large egg yolks
a small handful of almond flakes, toasted in a dry pan, to decorate

SERVES
12

ALMOND SPONGE

1. Preheat the oven to 160°C/325°F/Gas mark 3. Grease and line two 20 cm/8 in round sandwich tins. Use square tins if you'd prefer to serve the cake in fingers.

2. Beat the softened butter with the icing sugar until pale and fluffy. Add the eggs one at a time, beating well after each addition. Continue to beat until you have a slick mixture.

3. Tip in the ground almonds and fold everything together. The mixture should be a dropping consistency (so it falls easily from a spoon). Add a splash of milk if you need to loosen it.

4. Spread the batter into the tins and bake for about 25 minutes, or until the sponges are evenly browned on top and springy to the touch. Turn out onto a wire rack to cool, then pop them to chill in the fridge.

APRICOT AND ALMOND CAKE CONTINUED

APRICOT ICE CREAM

1. There is no need to skin the apricots. Stone them, chop them into small pieces and place in a saucepan with a splash of water and the sugar. Grind the cardamom seeds (if using) and add to the pan, then warm the fruit and sugar mixture over a medium heat.

2. Let the mixture bubble up, then turn down the heat and simmer for 15 minutes or so to drive off some of the water. If the fruit reaches a syrupy consistency before that, stop. Your aim is to create a runny compote.

3. Put aside 2 tbsp of the compote for the top of the cake. Add the milk and cream to the rest of the apricot mixture in the pan and warm through.

4. Beat the egg yolks together in a bowl, then take a tablespoon of the fruit and whisk it into the yolks. Add this egg mixture to the rest of the fruit and whisk it together. Stir the mixture over a gentle heat until it has thickened. The custard is ready when you notice a change in consistency on the back of your spoon. Leave to cool.

5. When the custard is cold, churn it in a machine, or stir-freeze: put the tub in your freezer, then every 30 minutes bring it out and mash the frozen edges with a fork, or use a hand blender to break up the ice crystals. You'll need to do this 3 or 4 times, until smooth and firm. Don't let the ice cream get too hard as you will need to spread it.

6. When you're ready to assemble the cake, bring out the cold sponge. Sandwich your ice cream in the middle. Decorate the top sponge with the toasted almond flakes, using the reserved apricot compote as glue.

7. Put the cake straight into the freezer on a suitable plate. Give it at least 3–4 hours in the freezer before you bring the cake back out to slice and serve.

HONEY AND TAHINI

I think of ancient Egypt when I taste this. Cleopatra would have loved it – probably in the bath. Roasted, crushed sesame paste gives a delicious savoury edge to the gorgeous honey.

375 ml/12½ fl oz/1½ cups whole milk
375 ml/12½ fl oz/1½ cups double cream
2 large eggs, plus 2 large yolks
240 g/9 oz/¾ cup honey
115 g/4 oz/½ cup tahini
a pinch of salt

MAKES
1.5 L

1. Put the milk and cream in a saucepan on a medium heat and bring to a simmer, being careful not to let the mixture catch on the bottom of the pan.

2. Whisk the eggs and yolks with the honey in a large bowl. Make sure it's all blended well.

3. Ladle the warm cream into the eggs and honey a little at a time, stirring well with each addition, until fully incorporated into the egg mixture. Tip this custard back into the pan, as long as the bottom is clean and not scorched.

4. Put the pan on a gentle heat and use a wooden spoon to keep the custard slowly moving as the heat thickens it. The custard is ready when you notice a change in consistency on the back of your spoon.

5. Measure the tahini into a bowl with a big pinch of salt. Add a little of the custard to the tahini and mix in well, then gradually add the rest until it has all come together. Tahini is very dense, so if you put too much custard in at once it'll go lumpy.

6. Taste, and add more salt if it doesn't immediately make you want to eat the lot right now. Leave the custard to cool completely.

7. When the custard is cold, churn in a machine or stir-freeze: put the tub in your freezer, then every 30 minutes bring it out and mash the frozen edges with a fork, or use a hand blender to break up the ice crystals. You'll need to do this 3 or 4 times, until smooth and firm.

8. Before serving, soften in the fridge for 10–15 minutes.

MONKEY GONE TO HEAVEN

This double award winner won a Northwest Fine Food award, and 'Best Dessert' at the British Street Food Awards, where I served it with hot toasted brioche. It's all the contrasts that make this so good: sweet and salty; smooth and textured.

I change the name depending on where I am. At a music festival, it's Monkey Gone to Heaven; at a producer's market or food festival, it's Roasted Banana, Salted Caramel and Peanut; near children it's Nutty Banana and Toffee. They're all true.

MAKES

1.5 L

SALTED CARAMEL

200 g/7 oz/generous ¾ cup sugar

40 g/1½ oz butter

200 ml/7 fl oz/scant 1 cup single cream

1 tsp sea salt flakes

BANANA ICE CREAM

350 g/12 oz banana flesh
  (about 3 very ripe, large fruit)

60 g/2¼ oz/¼ cup sugar

50 g/1¾ oz/generous ¼ cup icing sugar

1 tbsp lemon juice

a pinch of salt

6 tbsp milk

275 ml/9½ fl oz/scant 1¼ cups
  double cream

80 g/3¾ oz/¾ cup roasted peanuts
  (if salted, shake off excess salt)

SALTED CARAMEL

1. In a small pan, dissolve the sugar in 5 tbsp of water over a medium heat. Bring it to the boil, then watch it until it turns caramel in colour and smells of candy floss. Take the pan off the heat and add the butter. Stir in the cream very slowly so you avoid lumps. (If you get lumps, just put the pan back on a low heat and stir until they have melted.)

2. Add the salt. If you're using salted butter, use fewer salt flakes. Don't be shy, though – if you think it needs more salt for a proper caramel hit, do it. Let the caramel cool, then refrigerate.

BANANA ICE CREAM

1. Roast the banana or caramelise it in a pan (which is quicker). To roast, preheat the oven to 180°C/350°F/Gas mark 4. Place the whole, peeled bananas on a baking tray and roast for 30 minutes, until soft. Mix with the sugar and leave to cool. To caramelise, chop the bananas into thin discs and fry on a low heat with a little butter and the sugar until the discs are pulpy and catching at the edges; spread them across a plate. Chill in the fridge.

2. When the banana is cold, mix it with the icing sugar, lemon juice and a tiny pinch of salt. Pour in the milk and cream, give it a good stir and purée with a hand blender until smooth.

3. Churn in a machine; or stir-freeze, beating every 30–40 minutes. Don't let it set too hard before folding in the caramel and peanuts. Put the ice cream in a tub, spoon over the caramel, scatter the nuts, and fold. Before scooping, soften in the fridge for 20 minutes.

Make sure your bananas are really ripe, with their skins covered in black spots.

HAZELNUT AND WHITE TRUFFLE TERRINE

This flavour combination comes courtesy of French chef Pierre Hermé, and features in his macaroon collection. I created the recipe as soon as I left his shop on Rue Cambon, Paris, and it stopped me in my tracks. I had never tried truffle in a sweet dish before.

Silicone is the best mould for this ice cream – it's tough to remove the chocolate shell from anything else. I use a 1 litre/35 fl oz loaf-shaped one. If you don't have a mould, don't make a shell. Instead, churn the ice cream and, before it's stored in the freezer, drizzle over the cooled, melted chocolate and/or the chopped praline, *stracciatella* style. See the Garden Mint and Chocolate Crisp recipe (page 140) for the method.

SERVES
10

CHOCOLATE SHELL

250 g/9 oz milk chocolate, or
70 % cocoa-solids chocolate, chopped

PRALINE

70 g/2½ oz/⅓ cup caster sugar
40 g/1½ oz/⅓ cup roasted hazelnuts, roughly chopped

ICE CREAM

300 ml/10 fl oz/1¼ cups whole milk
300 ml/10 fl oz/1¼ cups double cream
140 g/5 oz/1 cup blanched and roasted hazelnuts, finely chopped
140 g/5 oz/generous ½ cup soft dark brown sugar
½ tsp white truffle oil

CHOCOLATE SHELL

1. Melt the chocolate in a heatproof bowl over a pan of barely simmering water. With a pastry brush, use half the chocolate to coat the inside of the mould to 5 cm/2 in up the sides, creating a good, thick layer. Pop the mould into the fridge to set for 10 minutes. Apply a second coat using the rest of the chocolate for a solid shell. Chill again.

PRALINE

1. Caramelise the sugar slowly in a dry pan (see page 81 for method). When it turns golden, pour it over a silicone mat and scatter over the nuts. When brittle, bash it into small bits.

ICE CREAM

1. Put the milk, cream, hazelnuts and sugar in a saucepan and, over a medium heat, bring the mixture to a simmer for 3 minutes, stirring to stop it catching. Turn off the heat and leave to infuse for 15 minutes. It should be fairly thick.

2. Blend briefly using a hand blender so the mixture is smooth but still has a nutty texture. Whisk in the white truffle oil and allow to cool.

3. When cold, churn in a machine, or stir-freeze, beating with a fork every 30 minutes. Scoop the finished ice cream into the chocolate mould, pressing with a spoon into the corners. Scatter the praline rubble over and lightly press in. Freeze for at least 4 hours. To serve, turn it onto a board and remove the mould, then cut into 2.5 cm/1 in) slices.

Truffle oil is pricey, but there's a wealth of other recipes you can use it in. Drizzle over pasta, roasted root vegetables, soups or avocado, or stir a drop into mayonnaise. If you don't want to splash out, don't use it – this will still be a sophisticated-tasting dessert.

PISTACHIO ICE CREAM TOASTED SANDWICHES

When I first visit any country, I can't wait to get to the food stores. Yes, for the fresh produce, but also for what's on the shelves in jars and cans – stuff that's probably as cheap and everyday as our marmalade and baked beans, but somehow seems exotic.

In Sicily I bought jars of pistachio spreads and pastes that looked like they were meant for toast. How decadent? I mixed some into a vanilla ice cream and fried it in buttered bread. This recipe uses whole nuts. Roasting or dry frying them brings out their best.

MAKES

1 L

PISTACHIO ICE CREAM

100 g/3½ oz/scant 1 cup shelled pistachios, whole

300 ml/10 fl oz/1¼ cups whole milk, plus 1 tbsp to make a paste

170 g/6 oz/scant ¾ cup sugar

450 ml/16 fl oz/scant 2 cups double cream

½ tsp sea salt flakes

2 tsp cornflour

SANDWICHES

2 thick slices of good-quality, day-old white bread for each sandwich

unsalted butter

mild olive oil

PISTACHIO ICE CREAM

1. Dry-fry the nuts in a large pan, until they release a nutty aroma. Toss them occasionally to stop them burning. When they have cooled a little, chop the nuts as finely as you can.

2. Put the milk, sugar and pistachios in a pan and bring to a simmer. Once the sugar has dissolved, remove from the heat. Use a hand blender to whiz into a thick, green mixture.

3. Return to the heat and add the cream and salt. Make a thin paste with the cornflour and the extra tablespoon of milk. Whisking the pistachio cream gently, pour in the cornflour paste. Keep slowly whisking over the heat until the mixture has thickened, about 5 minutes.

4. Let the pistachio cream cool completely, then churn in a machine, or stir-freeze: put the tub in your freezer, then every 30 minutes mash the frozen edges with a fork, until firm.

5. If you want to make the toasted sandwiches straightaway, let the ice cream harden in the freezer until it is firm enough to ball with an ice-cream scoop.

SANDWICHES

1. Cut your bread to accommodate 2 scoops per sandwich. Over a medium–low heat, melt a slice of butter in a frying pan with a drizzle of oil. Fry a round of bread on one side only, until golden. Remove from the pan, then fry the second round, this time with the ice cream on top. Put the first slice on top of the ice cream, and press down, squidging it all together.

If you make the custard for this ice cream the day before you churn it, the pistachio flavour will intensify overnight.

CANDIED CHESTNUT, VANILLA AND ROSEMARY

Chestnut and rosemary are very earthy, aren't they? Maybe not your first choice for an ice-cream flavour? But put vanilla in the middle, grabbing both by the hands to skip merrily together into the churner, singing "Come on, guys! We can do this!" and you've got an utterly delicious scoop. It's nutty, floral, and slightly treacle-y as a result of the caramelisation.

MAKES

1 L

ICE CREAM

400 ml/14 fl oz/1¾ cups whole milk, plus extra for making a cornflour paste

300 ml/10 fl oz/1¼ cups double cream

180 g/6¼ oz/½ cup sugar

½ split vanilla pod, or ½ tsp vanilla extract

1 bushy sprig of rosemary about 10 cm/4 in long

1 tbsp cornflour

CANDIED CHESTNUTS

a knob of butter

2 heaped tbsp soft brown sugar

2 tbsp Crème de Châtaigne (or other nutty liqueur), or 1 tbsp water

120 g/4¼ oz/1 cup chestnuts, chopped

a good pinch of sea salt

ICE CREAM

1. Slowly heat the milk, cream, sugar, vanilla and rosemary in a pan and bring to a boil. Gently simmer for 10 minutes, stirring from time to time.

2. Make a paste with a splash of milk and the cornflour and whisk it into the pan. Whisk until thickened, then strain to remove the rosemary and vanilla pod (if using). Cool.

3. When the custard is cold, churn in a machine, or stir-freeze: put the tub in your freezer, then every 30 minutes mash the frozen edges with a fork, until smooth and firm.

CANDIED CHESTNUTS

1. Melt the butter and sugar over a medium heat. Add the liqueur or 1 tbsp of water and let it bubble. To mix, swirl the pan, but don't stir.

2. Add the chestnuts and poach in the syrup for 5 minutes. Crunch in the sea salt before tipping the lot onto a plate to go cold.

3. When the ice cream is set to a soft consistency, fold in the chestnut mix and return straight to the freezer. Before scooping, soften in the fridge for 15–20 minutes.

KILLER VANILLA WITH APRICOT KERNEL

Becoming conscious of how much alcohol I throw into things for extra flavour, I ditched the Disaronno in my apricot ice-cream recipe, deciding to add flavour with the fruit stones instead. Then I remembered something about the kernels being toxic with cyanide – so much for my new, conscientious approach! I did some research: using eight kernels per litre of milk is well below any dangerous level. I like the kind of pleasure/pain tension that's at work here and in other edgy foodstuffs such as oysters, chillies, or pufferfish, which served incorrectly can be poisonous. How good can a fish taste that you'd risk that?

The title, you understand, is entirely tongue in cheek, and not tongue-swelling and turning blue. I wouldn't poison my customers, I love them dearly.

8 apricot stones
350 ml/12 fl oz/1½ cups whole milk
300 ml/10 fl oz/1¼ cups double cream
½ vanilla pod
6 egg yolks
170 g/6 oz/scant ¾ cup sugar
a pinch of salt (optional)

MAKES

1 L

1. To release the flavour from the apricot stones, smash them with something heavy. I use the base of my granite mortar. You'll see the white, nutty kernel inside. Add all the broken pieces (outer shell and inner kernel) to the milk and double cream in a large saucepan.

2. Split and scrape the seeds from the vanilla pod and add the pod and seeds to the pan. Bring to boiling point. Simmer for 2 minutes, gently stirring, then turn off the heat and leave the flavours to infuse for 15 minutes.

3. Beat the egg yolks and sugar in a bowl until pale and foamy. Strain the milk and cream and discard the apricot bits, then pour the liquid straight into the yolk mixture. Return to the pan and stir on a gentle heat until the custard has thickened. The custard is ready when you notice a change in consistency on the back of your spoon. Give it a taste; you should get an almond flavour coming through. If it's not pronounced enough, add a little pinch of salt. Leave the custard to cool down.

4. When the custard is cold, churn in a machine, or stir-freeze: put the tub in your freezer, then every 30 minutes bring it out and mash the frozen edges with a fork, or use a hand blender to break up the ice crystals. You'll need to do this 3 or 4 times, until smooth and firm.

5. Before serving, soften for 20 minutes in the fridge.

You can buy bags of apricot kernels from wholefood stores. However, because they're not as fresh, you might need to use up to 15 kernels for the flavour to come through.

PEANUT BUTTER AND SALTED CARAMEL

I once wrote on Facebook that there wasn't anything in the world that couldn't be improved by adding peanut butter. Loads of comments followed. I eat it most mornings with half an avocado, but favourite ways are to stick my finger into a jar of peanut butter and then into a bag of raisins; and to sandwich it between two After Eight mints. Try it. Do. Thank me later.

In this recipe, the peanut butter is a great foil to rich caramel – you get that thrilling salt-sweet buzz on your tongue.

This is a variation on my recipe that has Mancunians queuing down the street. It's insanely moreish and totally bad for you.

900 ml/30 fl oz/3¾ cups single cream
240 g/9 oz/1 cup soft light brown sugar
1 tsp table salt (or up to 2 tsp sea salt flakes)
150 g/5½ oz/½ cup crunchy peanut butter

MAKES

1 L

1. To make the caramel sauce, warm 600 ml/20 fl oz/2½ cups of the single cream on a medium heat to just below boiling point. Stir in the brown sugar and salt, and when it's a nice, smooth consistency, let the sauce cool.

2. Mix the caramel into the peanut butter, a little at a time to prevent lumps, and then whisk in the rest of the cream (or 300 ml/10 fl oz/1¼ cups of milk, if you prefer something lighter). Let it go completely cold in the fridge.

3. Churn in a machine, or stir-freeze: put the tub in your freezer, then every 30 minutes bring it out and mash the frozen edges with a fork, or use a hand blender to break up the ice crystals. You'll need to do this 3 or 4 times, until the ice cream is smooth and firm.

4. Leave this just a few minutes to soften at room temperature before you scoop.

CORIANDER LEAF

It's a fragile soul with a gentle nature, the coriander leaf. My heart sinks when a client on a food styling shoot wants to finish a plate with it to denote freshness. Unlike its perky cousin parsley, coriander droops and clings to the plate. Its flavour is also volatile. With heat it dies quickly, which is why it's mainly used as a garnish.

Here, we add coriander to cold milk at the end of cooking to keep its fresh, grassy, wood-and-earth aroma. I love it despite its gentle nature, like a fey but catchy folk song.

50 g/1¾ oz fresh coriander sprigs
400 ml/14 fl oz/1¾ cups whole milk
400 ml/14 fl oz/1¾ cups double cream
zest of 1 large unwaxed lemon
200 g/7 oz/generous ¾ cup sugar
5 tsp cornflour

MAKES

1 L

1. Tear the leaves and topmost parts of the stalks off the coriander sprigs and set aside. Combine the milk and cream in a measuring jug. Pour half the liquid into a saucepan with the lemon zest and bring to a rolling simmer. After a minute, turn down the heat and stir in the sugar.

2. Make a paste with the cornflour, using a little of the reserved milk and cream mixture.

3. Pour the paste slowly into the pan, stirring all the time to prevent lumps. Continue stirring for 2–3 minutes until the custard has thickened. The custard is ready when you notice a change in consistency on the back of your spoon. Transfer to a large bowl to cool.

4. Drop the coriander leaves into the remaining cold milk and cream, and briefly pulse with a hand blender for just a few seconds. The liquid will be pale green and flecked.

5. When the custard has cooled, gently whisk the two creams together.

6. When the mix is completely cold, pop it into the fridge to chill. Churn in a machine, or stir-freeze: put the tub in your freezer, then every 30 minutes bring it out and mash the frozen edges with a fork, or use a hand blender to break up the ice crystals. You'll need to do this 3 or 4 times, until smooth and firm.

7. Soften in the fridge for 15–20 minutes before serving.

CITRUS CINNAMON BRÛLÉE

Burning sugar is like alchemy. I find it fascinating to watch white granules dissolve into clear liquid, then transform by degrees into caramel – the confectionery all-rounder with a million uses. We're making caramel shards for this ice cream. Your first bash of brittle amber-sweet will splinter into admirable slivers of gold, so bash it further to make softer rubble, like the topping of crème brûlée.

I fold the crunchy caramel topping through the finished ice cream. The pieces of caramelised sugar soften in the freshly churned ice cream. If you prefer to leave them out of the mix, you can sprinkle them on top of scoops instead.

MAKES

1 L

CARAMEL BRÛLÉE
70 g/2½ oz/scant ⅓ cup caster sugar

ICE CREAM
500 ml/18 fl oz/2 cups whole milk

500 ml/18 fl oz/2 cups double cream

1 tsp ground cinnamon

zest of 1 unwaxed lemon, to taste

100 g/3½ oz/scant ½ cup dark
brown sugar

10 large egg yolks

1. First caramelise the sugar for the brûlée. Use a thick-based pan that distributes heat well. Cover the bottom of the pan in an even layer of sugar, put it over a low heat, and wait. Don't touch it. When the sugar starts to break down and you can see it changing colour, give the pan a swirl but don't stir the mixture with a spoon. (Sugar is temperamental.) Once it has turned into an even amber-coloured liquid, pour it onto a silicone mat or greased baking parchment. When cold and brittle, bash it up into pieces.

2. Pour the milk and cream into a pan and add the cinnamon and lemon zest. Heat until the mixture reaches boiling point. Turn off the heat and let the flavours infuse for 15 minutes.

3. Beat the sugar and egg yolks until light and frothy. Strain the milk slowly into the eggs and sugar, stopping to mix at intervals. I find it easiest to strain the milk first into a measuring jug, then pour and stir.

4. As long as the milk and cream didn't catch on the bottom, return the mixture to the original saucepan and slowly stir it over a gentle heat to thicken the custard. The custard is ready when you notice a change in consistency on the back of your spoon.

5. When it is completely cold, churn the mix in a machine, or stir-freeze: put the tub in your freezer, then every 30 minutes bring it out and mash the frozen edges with a fork, or use a hand blender to break up the ice crystals. You'll need to do this 3 or 4 times, until smooth and firm. Fold in the sugar pieces towards the end of churning, so that they become suspended in the ice cream.

6. Soften in the fridge for 10–15 minutes before scooping.

CHOCOLATE AND GINGER TERRINE

This recipe isn't difficult, but it requires juggling a few bowls: have four to hand. Reserve the biggest bowl for the cream – this is where you combine the ingredients. This is a good dessert if you're having people round, and it's popular with kids.

NO CHURN

MAKES
8–10
SLICES

200 g/7 oz ginger biscuits, crushed

a small splash of brandy, or any liqueur (optional)

3 large eggs, separated

100 g/3½ oz/generous ⅓ cup caster sugar

3 pieces preserved stem ginger, finely chopped, plus 6 tbsp syrup from the jar

100 g/3½ oz milk chocolate, broken up

300 ml/10 fl oz/1¼ cups double cream

1. Use a 900 ml/31 fl oz silicone loaf tin, or line a metal tin with a double layer of cling film.

2. Mix the biscuits with the liqueur, if using, and cover the base of the tin with half of the biscuit mix. Put this first layer of the terrine into the freezer.

3. Whisk the egg yolks, sugar and 2 tbsp of the ginger syrup in a heatproof bowl and place over a pan of simmering water for 3–4 minutes. Keep whisking to create a thick, pale, custard-like sauce, called a sabayon. Remove the bowl from the pan and set aside.

4. Pop the chocolate into another bowl and put this over the simmering water to melt.

5. Whisk the egg whites until they hold their shape. In your largest bowl, whip the double cream until it forms soft peaks. Fold the egg whites into the cream. Then fold the sabayon into the cream. Give it all a good turn around the bowl, being careful not to knock out too much air.

6. Divide this mixture into 2 bowls. (You should have empty bowls on the work surface – just re-use them.)

7. To make the next layer of the terrine, fold the melted chocolate into one bowl of mixture. Take the terrine tin out of the freezer and add in the chocolate ice cream, then pop it back into the freezer.

8. To the other bowl, add 4 tbsp of ginger syrup and the chopped ginger. Give it all a good stir.

9. Take the terrine tin out again and scatter over the second half of the biscuit crumbs. Then add the white ginger layer, which is the last. Freeze for at least 4 hours.

10. The heat from your hands should loosen the terrine from its tin when it is time to turn it out. Cut the terrine into 2.5 cm/1 in slices to serve.

BLACKBERRY AND STAR ANISE SORBET

For want of a better description, this is a very grown-up sorbet. Not too sweet, deep and darkly fruity, it tastes almost like a frozen Crème de Mûre.

Fresh berries can be expensive to buy, so go foraging along hedgerows if you can. Wear something to protect your legs from brambles and give the fruit a good rinse when you get home. You'll notice that wild fruit is sweeter than the ubiquitous supermarket berry when you eat it in season. A little of this sorbet goes a long way; so halve the ingredients if you prefer.

6 star anise
150 g/5½ oz/scant ⅔ cup sugar
9 tbsp liquid glucose
500 g/1 lb 2 oz fresh blackberries

MAKES

1 L

1. Put the star anise in a pan with 1 litre/35 fl oz/4 cups of water and bring to a boil, then reduce the heat and simmer for 10 minutes.

2. Put the sugar into a bowl and pour the glucose over it. Pour 500 ml/18 fl oz/2 cups of the hot water from the pan onto the sugar and glucose, and give it a good stir. Discard the remaining hot water, along with the star anise.

3. Return the liquid to a very low heat and add the blackberries. Let the fruit gently poach in the sugar syrup for 5 minutes, making sure all the sugar and glucose have dissolved.

4. Blitz the mixture with a hand blender. When it's smooth, strain the liquid into a bowl through a fine sieve to remove any roughage. Leave to cool completely. To speed up the process, you can suspend the bowl in a larger bowl of ice-cold water.

5. When it has completely cooled, chill the sorbet mix in the fridge. Churn in a machine, or stir-freeze: put the tub in your freezer, then every 30 minutes bring it out and mash the frozen edges with a fork, or use a hand blender to break up the ice crystals. You'll need to do this 3 or 4 times, until smooth and firm.

6. Before serving, soften in the fridge for 10 minutes.

This intensely flavoured sorbet marries perfectly with a hot apple crumble. But apple and blackberry are by no means exclusive – you could give the berry a wild fling with pineapple upside-down cake; and white chocolate cheesecake makes a seductive bit on the side.

MASTIC ICE CREAM WITH EASY BAKLAVA

Musky, strange, spicy and slightly chewy. I have a customer from the Greek island of Chios, where the pistachio tree is cultivated for its resin – mastic. It forms crystals, and is harvested for a variety of uses, including culinary. Georgios offers me all sorts of weird ingredients to try, and I admit I was a bit unsure of the mastic. Then he referred me to a recipe from Greek chef Tessa Kiros, which is pretty much how I've listed it here. The ice cream tastes like authentic Turkish delight. A drop of rose essence is a nice addition, but if you haven't tasted mastic on its own, I recommend it. When I first tried mastic, I couldn't imagine the flavour having any merit. Honestly, though, this is a stunning dessert.

In a holistic move, I've paired this ice cream with pistachio-dusted honeyed filo pastry. The deep muskiness of mastic is a perfect foil for very sweet things.

MAKES
0.5 L

SERVES
6

MASTIC ICE CREAM

½ tsp mastic powder, or 1 tsp mastic crystals, finely ground
85 g/3 oz/⅓ cup sugar
200 ml/7 fl oz/scant 1 cup whole milk
200 ml/7 fl oz/scant 1 cup double cream

BAKLAVA

75 g/2½ oz/scant ½ cup icing sugar, sifted
6 sheets filo pastry
125 g/4½ oz butter, melted
70 g/2½ oz/½ cup pistachios, roughly chopped
70 g/2½ oz/½ cup almonds, roughly chopped

HONEY SYRUP

100 g/3½ oz/scant ⅓ cup honey, runny or set
zest and juice of ½ an unwaxed lemon
crushed seeds from 4 cardamom pods

MASTIC ICE CREAM

1. Mix the mastic into the sugar; don't be tempted to use more than half a teaspoon, which is plenty. Pour the cold milk into a saucepan and add the sugar and mastic mix, stirring until it has dissolved. Put the pan on the heat and bring to a simmer, stirring with a balloon whisk. (If your mastic is in crystal form, grind it, then mix it with the sugar and add to the milk.)

2. Let the milk simmer for a couple of minutes, whisking. Allow it to cool completely. To speed up the process, pour it into a cold bowl and sit this in a larger bowl of ice-cold water.

3. When the mastic-flavoured milk is cold, stir in the cream and refrigerate for 1 hour. Then churn in a machine, or stir-freeze, remembering to beat the ice cream with a fork every 30 minutes, until firm. Before it completely hardens, you can also use a hand blender or food processor to get an ultra-smooth consistency.

Mastic can be found in Greek or Middle Eastern shops and supermarkets, or ordered in small quantities online.

BAKLAVA

1. Heat the oven to 180°C/350°F/Gas mark 4. Put the sifted icing sugar into a large bowl.

2. Roll up the sheets of filo and cut into discs of about 1 cm/½ in wide, to create ribbons of pastry that look like tagliatelle pasta. Tip them into the icing sugar and gently run them through your fingers to coat with the sugar.

3. Spread the strips across a lipped baking sheet or oven dish, and spoon the melted butter evenly over the top. Toss the chopped nuts over the pastry. Bake in the oven until the top is browned, about 15 minutes.

HONEY SYRUP

1. Put all the ingredients in a saucepan with 4 tbsp of water and bring to a gentle boil.

2. When the pastry comes out of the oven, spoon the syrup over the top and leave the whole thing to cool and firm up a little. It will have quite a loose texture even when cool and lend itself to eating with a spoon.

3. Soften the ice cream in the fridge for 10 minutes. Serve a generous scoop with a mound of the still-warm pastry.

LIQUORICE ROOT

For a delicate liquorice taste that's woody and herby, try to find some root sticks to use in this ice cream. They are inexpensive and readily available in wholefood stores. Having already used an intense liquorice extract, I was initially disappointed with the taste of the real thing. But when it came out of the churner, I was bowled over by how unusually delicious it is. This recipe produces something silky smooth.

450 ml/16 fl oz/scant 2 cups whole milk, plus a little extra to make a paste

375 ml/12½ fl oz/generous 1½ cups double cream

6–8 liquorice roots, 13–15 cm/5–6 in long

135 g/5 oz/generous ½ cup soft brown sugar

¼ tsp salt

2 rounded tbsp cornflour

MAKES

1 L

1. Bring the milk, cream and liquorice sticks just up to boiling point in a saucepan, then turn off the heat. The sticks will now be softer; remove them from the pan and chop into small pieces to release more flavour. If they splinter horizontally, even better.

2. Stir the pieces back into the milk and cream and add the sugar and salt. Leave it to infuse for up to an hour. Strain the liquid through a fine sieve, so that all the little splinters from the sticks are gone.

3. Make a thin paste with the cornflour and a little milk. Pour the cornflour paste into the liquorice milk and warm it over a medium heat, whisking to prevent lumps. Stop whisking when the liquid has thickened.

4. Let the mixture cool, and then chill in the fridge. Churning in a machine gives the very best results for this silky ice cream, but stir-freezing is okay, as long as you remember that once you've put the tub in your freezer, every 30 minutes you must mash the frozen edges with a fork, until smooth and firm.

This is a great ice cream for Hallowe'en – it's got a Gothic ring to it, like some ingredient in a witch's brew.

MELON AND CHILLI

Cashews – a fabulous and ingenious way to make a creamy, smooth vegan ice cream. You just need to properly break them down in a blender to release their dairy-esque goodness.

Chilli is a personal thing – only you know how much to put in. Me, I use a quarter of a bird's eye chilli – with seeds, because I like to live dangerously. No matter how scorchio you make it, cold ice cream and cool refreshing melon will soothe the tongue. In fact, you don't notice the heat until later. I get many a tough guy order a chilli ice cream at the van, giving out that it isn't hot enough, only to see him pull that 'whoo-oo' face when he's walking away. Tut.

240 g/9 oz/generous 1½ cups unsalted cashews

1 average-size, ripe cantaloupe melon, about 600 g/1 lb 5 oz, chopped small

120 g/4½ oz/¾ cup icing sugar

1 bird's eye chilli, to taste

juice of 2 limes, to taste

VEGAN   MAKES 1 L

1. Use a hand blender or food processor to blitz the cashews thoroughly.

2. Mix the melon, nuts and icing sugar together in a bowl with as much chilli as you want to use, then blend in a liquidiser, or use a hand blender. Keep blending for 3–4 minutes, until the mixture is smooth, glossy and soupy.

3. Strain the mixture through a fine sieve. Use the limes to season – the amount of juice in limes varies wildly, so taste as you go, aiming to balance the sweetness. Melons can be so sweet that you might use both limes, but be careful not to let them overpower the other flavours.

4. Chill the mixture in the fridge and then churn in a machine, or stir-freeze: put the tub in your freezer, then every 30 minutes bring it out and mash the frozen edges with a fork, or use a hand blender to break up the ice crystals. You'll need to do this 3 or 4 times, until smooth and firm.

5. Before serving, this ice cream needs a good 10–15 minutes at room temperature to soften.

GINGER (OR STRAWBERRY BLONDE)

It can be tricky to get the flavour of real ginger into ice cream, as the root contains an enzyme that curdles milk. As long as you stick to my measurements, this ice cream will work, delivering a clean ginger taste.

Another good recipe uses stem ginger. Follow the vanilla recipe on page 16, but substitute stem ginger syrup for half the sugar, and add some chopped nuggets while the ice cream is soft. Tasty, but not the real thing ... it would probably call itself strawberry blonde.

My mate Vic, a redhead, decided while we were at a festival that it was time to reclaim the word 'ginger' for redheads. It had, we agreed, become unnecessarily derisory. So she set off around the festival, offering half-price ice cream to proud gingers. The following response made me laugh:

Vic: "Excuse me, sir, would you call yourself a ginger?"
Sir: "Well, no, I'm strawberry blonde."
Vic: "Oh, I'm sorry. I can't help you."
Sir: "Er ... oh."

400 ml/14 fl oz/1¾ cups whole milk
400 ml/14 fl oz/1¾ cups double cream
5 cm/2 in root ginger
6 large egg yolks
180 g/6¼ oz/¾ cup sugar
a big pinch of sea salt flakes

MAKES
1 L

1. Put the milk and cream together in a saucepan. Scrape the outer skin from the ginger then grate it (use a Microplane grater if you have one) into the pan. Stir it over a medium heat. When it just comes to a simmer and you see bubbles rising round the edges, turn off the heat and leave it to infuse for 5 minutes.

2. Whisk the egg yolks, sugar and sea salt together in a bowl, then strain the ginger cream through a fine sieve into the yolks and mix it all thoroughly.

3. Return this mixture to the pan on a low heat, whisking slowly so the eggs do not scramble. Stop when the mixture thickens. The custard is ready when you notice a change in consistency on the back of your spoon.

4. Leave the custard to cool completely before churning in a machine, or stir-freezing. Put the tub in your freezer, then every 30 minutes bring it out and mash the frozen edges with a fork, or use a hand blender to break up the ice crystals. You'll need to do this 3 or 4 times, until smooth and firm.

5. Before serving, soften in the fridge for 10 minutes.

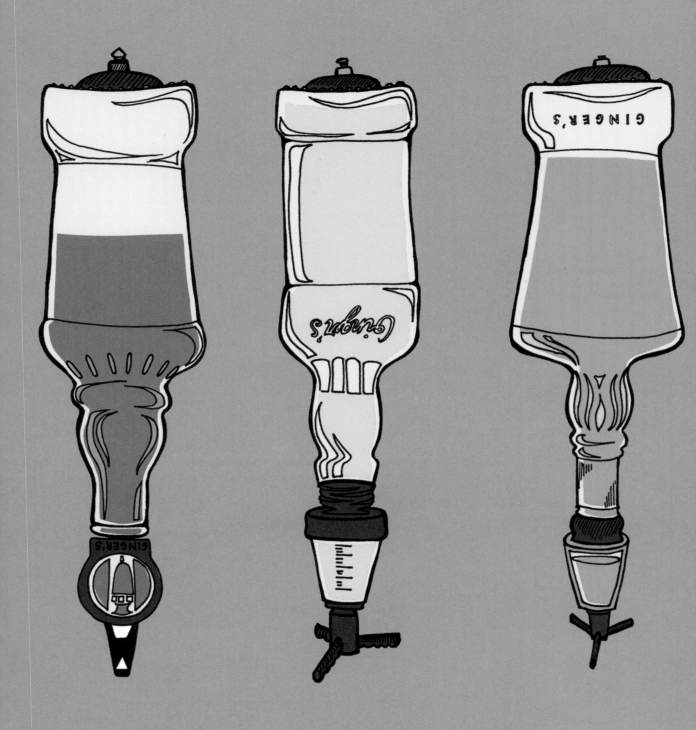

BOOZY

DARK AND STORMY

Like the cocktail of the same name, this balances dark rum, lime and ginger. Cocktail menus are a brilliant source of inspiration. Mixologists deal in flavour alchemy – you can trust them.

You can whip up this easy, no-churn recipe in 10 minutes, and then fling it into the freezer and forget about it until you want to eat it.

130 g/4½ oz/scant 1 cup icing sugar
juice and zest of 1 unwaxed lime
6 tbsp rum
5 nuggets stem ginger, plus 6 tbsp syrup from the jar
500 ml/18 fl oz/2 cups double cream

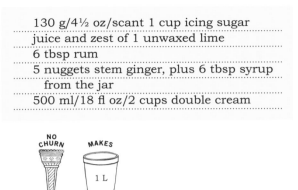

NO CHURN   MAKES 1 L

1. In a large bowl, mix together the icing sugar, 2 tbsp of the lime juice, and the lime zest, rum and ginger syrup. Save the whole ginger pieces for the end stage. If your kitchen is really warm, you might want to pop this mixture into the fridge for 15 minutes – it needs to be cold so that the cream will whip up properly.

2. Pour the cream into the ginger and lime mix, and whisk until you have soft peaks that hold for a few seconds, before flopping back into the bowl.

3. Chop the nuggets of stem ginger into tiny pieces or slivers, and fold them into the cream. Turn it all into a tub and pop the ice cream into the freezer.

4. This ice cream is quite scoopable straight from the freezer, so you may need only a few minutes' notice to serve it. Try it served with doughnuts (page 170), which take no time at all, and turn this into a sort of rum baba.

If you can't get a jar of stem ginger, substitute 200 g/7 oz ginger jam for the nuggets and syrup, and add it in the first step with the icing sugar, lime and rum. Ginger jam is widely available.

GRAPPA AND BLUEBERRY

A family holiday in Sicily and a fantastic find – a tiny trattoria doing authentic dishes with a real Nonna (grandma) in the kitchen. At the end of our meal we were handed a sort of perfume aerosol filled with grappa and told to spray it into our mouths as a digestif. I'm not man enough to spray this spirit straight onto my tongue but it gave me an idea … a spritz of this across a slice of lemon and polenta cake – *che bello!* I like something harsh against sweetness. It lengthens and heightens the experience.

250 g/9 oz blueberries
160 g/5½ oz/scant ⅔ cup sugar
280 ml/9½ fl oz/scant 1¼ cups double cream
3 tbsp grappa (35–42 % volume)

NO CHURN

MAKES

1 L

1. Simmer the blueberries in a saucepan with the sugar and 3 tbsp of water for 10 minutes. Push the fruit compote through a fine sieve into a bowl to remove any bits and then leave to cool completely. To speed up the cooling, spread the compote out in a large tin.

2. Whip the cream with the grappa until it forms soft peaks, then fold in the cold blueberry compote until a soft mass of dark purple cream emerges. Scoop this into a container and pop it into the freezer. There is no need to churn or stir the ice cream as it sets, just freeze it for at least 4 hours, or preferably overnight.

3. Before serving, soften the ice cream in the fridge for 10–15 minutes. The alcohol content will keep it soft, but the high water content of the fruit can make it icy if it's too cold. When it's ready to serve, it will be lovely and smooth.

Grappa is a distinctive brandy made from the 'pomace' of used grape skin, seeds and stems, after winemaking. Grapes – the gift that keeps on giving! If you don't have grappa, use a good-quality brandy.

IRISH CREAM LIQUEUR ICE CREAM

Is this a festive drink for everyone? The first aroma of Irish cream liqueur in the season makes me feel sad. I can put this down only to association with a bad Christmas past – perhaps the one during which I drank a bottle to myself over a week, then couldn't zip up my jeans. It's all too easy to knock back this Irish cream. Having it as an ice cream gives you more time to savour.

3 large eggs, separated
100 g/3½ oz/generous ⅓ cup sugar
120 ml/4 fl oz/½ cup Irish cream liqueur
500 ml/18 fl oz/2 cups double cream

NO CHURN   MAKES   1 L

1. Whisk the yolks, sugar and Irish cream liqueur in a heatproof bowl and place the bowl on a pan of gently simmering water. Keep whisking to cook the yolks, taking care to keep the mixture moving, until it is thick and pale. The custard is ready when you notice a change in consistency on the back of your spoon. Leave to cool.

2. Whip the cream to soft peaks in a bowl and then do the same in a separate bowl with the egg whites. Fold the cream and egg whites together and set aside.

3. When the yolk mixture is cold, fold it into the combined cream and egg whites.

4. Freeze for at least 4 hours, or preferably overnight. I recommend serving a scoop in a strong, hot black coffee (ideally, an espresso), affogato-style.

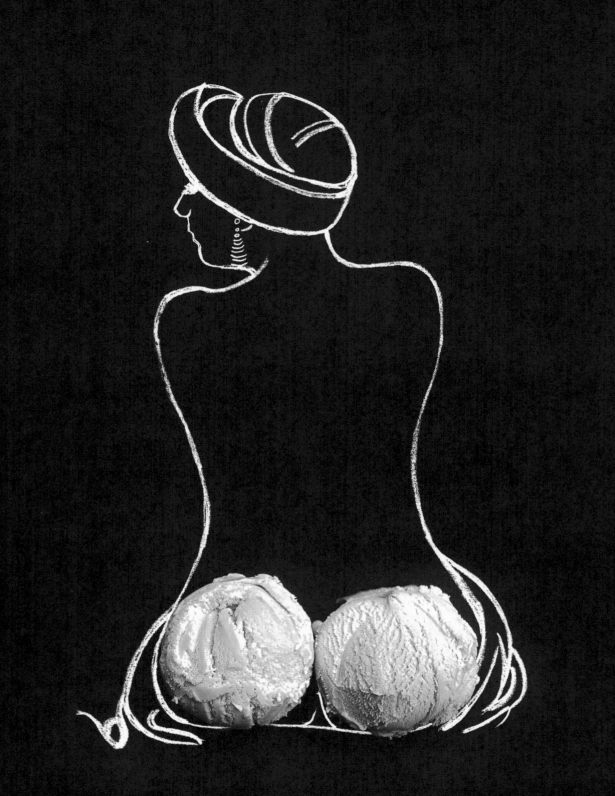

CHOCOLATE, RED WINE, CLOVE AND BLACK PEPPER

Slowly does this recipe. A low heat and a gentle stir is all you need. So pour a glass of Shiraz and enjoy your cooking.

I put this together on a cold January evening, after a New Year's party had left dregs of some spicy red wine hanging about, and influences of Christmas Glühwein were still in my mind.

350 ml/12 fl oz/1½ cups red wine, a Shiraz if you have it
1½ tbsp whole black peppercorns
1 tsp whole cloves
a few star anise
a few shavings of orange zest
170 g/6 oz/scant ¾ cup sugar
2 tbsp liquid glucose
6 tsp cocoa powder
200 ml/7 fl oz/scant 1 cup whole milk
140 g/5 oz Ecuadorian dark chocolate, 85 % cocoa-solids, finely chopped
6 large egg yolks
350 ml/12 fl oz/1½ cups double cream

MAKES

1 L

1. Mix the red wine with the aromatics, sugar and glucose in a pan on your lowest heat setting. Let it warm gently, stirring until the sugar has melted away. Leave on this low heat for 10 minutes to let the spices infuse; don't let it bubble too much.

2. Make a smooth paste from the cocoa and milk. Add this to the pan and cook this mixture for 5–6 minutes, slowly moving it around to stop it catching on the bottom. Take it off the heat, strain out the aromatics and add half the chocolate to the strained liquid (the other half goes in as chunks later). Leave this to melt, then whisk the mixture until it is smooth.

3. Return the spiced chocolate mixture to a saucepan. Beat the egg yolks a little in a bowl and then ladle a small amount of the chocolate mixture into the yolks. Add this back into the pan and cook on a gentle heat, stirring well, until the custard becomes slightly thicker. The custard is ready when you notice a change in consistency on the back of your spoon.

4. Take the pan off the heat and cool completely. Then add the cream. Chill in the fridge until completely cold.

5. Churn in a machine, folding through the remaining chocolate before you store the ice cream in the freezer. Or to stir-freeze, put the tub in your freezer, then every 30 minutes bring it out and mash the frozen edges with a fork, or use a hand blender to break up the ice crystals. You'll need to do this 3 or 4 times, until smooth and firm, but fold in the rest of the chocolate before the mixture gets too hard.

6. Soften for 15 minutes in the fridge before serving.

REAL ALE SORBET SHANDY

This is a different and refreshing way to enjoy beer – and it's ridiculously simple to knock together. Serve this scooped into a long glass of lemonade on a sunny day.

500 ml/18 fl oz/2 cups bitter ale (I use a good old Kentish brew, Spitfire)
75 g/2½ oz/scant ½ cup icing sugar

MAKES

0.5 L

1. Pour a little of the beer into the icing sugar to make a paste. Continue adding the beer, whisking as you go, to dissolve all the sugar.

2. Churn in a machine, or stir-freeze: put the tub in your freezer, then every 30 minutes mash the frozen edges with a fork, until smooth and firm. This will scoop straight from the freezer.

MOJITO CREAM WHITE RUM, LIME AND MINT

An invigorating take on the popular and refreshing cocktail. If you don't have mint extract and prefer to use fresh, take the leaves from a bushy bunch and use a food processor to blitz them into the sugar. I love the quick ease of this recipe – five minutes from start to finish.

zest and juice of 2 unwaxed limes
4 tsp icing sugar
1 tsp mint extract, or 10 g/½ oz fresh mint leaves, blitzed
7 tbsp white rum, such as Bacardi
600 ml/20 fl oz/generous 2½ cups double cream

MAKES
1 L

1. Put the lime zest and juice into a large bowl. Add the sugar, mint extract (or blitzed fresh mint leaves) and rum and blend with a fork. Pour in the cream (the colder it is, the easier it is to whip) and whisk with an electric whisk until soft peaks form.

2. Taste the mixture and add a dash of extra lime or one more teaspoon of rum if needed. Pour into a tub and freeze overnight.

3. This should scoop with relative ease straight from the freezer.

CHRISTMAS PUD ICE CREAM

Uptake of traditional Christmas pudding after a big Christmas dinner is quite low in our house. We see it as a sort of patriotic act to get through a dense wedge of rich pud – a bit like the Queen's speech, which some of us just aren't up for.

I do love the stuff, though. In fact, I've been known to live off it (I'd been styling Christmas pudding for a supermarket shoot and had tons of the stuff). But, who could say no to a bowl of Christmas pud ice cream? It's much lighter but with all the rich taste.

130 g/4½ oz/1 cup mixed dried fruit
1 tbsp zest from an unwaxed orange
6 tbsp brandy
130 g/4½ oz/⅔ cup icing sugar
1 tbsp lemon juice
500 ml/18 fl oz/2 cups double cream
230 g/8 oz Christmas pudding, crumbled

NO CHURN

MAKES

1.5 L

1. Soak the dried fruit and orange zest in the brandy for 1 hour. I microwave the pudding to heat it, then crumble it and let it cool – I find the texture is less greasy this way. There may be no need, and it may just be the puddings I buy. They are already cooked, after all – entirely up to you.

2. Mix the icing sugar, lemon juice, brandied fruit and soaking liqueur in a bowl. Add the cream (make sure it's cold to help whipping) and whip to soft peaks.

3. Reserve 30 g/1 oz of the pudding pieces, and fold the rest through the cream mix. Pour the mix into a 1.5 litre/52 fl oz loaf tin, or a pudding basin (see tip, below). Decorate by crumbling the reserved pudding over the top.

4. Freeze overnight – there is no need to stir-freeze, just let it set. Dip the loaf tin or basin in warm water for a few seconds to release the ice cream. Your icy Christmas pud should be soft enough to scoop within minutes.

Set the ice cream in a pudding basin to keep it real, and decorate with some holly when you've turned it out. Tacky? Yes. Merry Christmas.

GUINNESS AND GINGERBREAD

This can be enjoyed in so many ways.
The bitter maltiness works well with cola
– so drop in a scoop to make a cola float.
Chocolate cake is a great partner, too, or try
a toasted fruitcake. All foods want a piece of
Mr Guinness and Gingerbread – he has the
most fun times.

440ml can Guinness
250 ml/9 fl oz/1 cup double cream
300 ml/10 fl oz/1¼ cups whole milk
1 level tsp ground ginger
a pinch of salt
125 g/4½ oz/½ cup dark brown sugar
50 g/1¾ oz/scant ¼ cup white sugar
4 tsp cornflour

MAKES

1 L

1. Reserve 80 ml/2¾ fl oz/scant ⅓ cup of the Guinness and pour the rest into a saucepan.
    Over a medium heat, boil until reduced to about a quarter of its volume (6 tbsp), about
    10 minutes. Set aside.

2. In another pan, gently heat the double cream with 250 ml/9 fl oz/1 cup of the milk.
    Mix the ginger, salt and both sugars in a bowl, then add to the pan and whisk into the
    cream and milk. On a low heat, simmer for a couple of minutes while stirring.

3. Blend the cornflour into the remaining milk, using a fork to avoid lumps. Whisk this into
    the pan. Turn up the heat a little and cook, stirring well, until the mixture has thickened,
    about 2–3 minutes. The custard is ready when you notice a change in consistency on the
    back of your spoon. Leave to cool.

4. When cold, whisk in the reduced Guinness and the reserved Guinness.

5. Churn the mixture in a machine, or stir-freeze: put the tub in your freezer, then every
    30 minutes bring it out and mash the frozen edges with a fork, or use a hand blender to
    break up the ice crystals. You'll need to do this 3 or 4 times, until smooth and firm.

6. Before serving, soften in the fridge for 10 minutes.

If you use a saucepan with a pouring lip to reduce the Guinness, you can quickly check whether or not you've
reduced enough by pouring it into a measuring jug without risk of spillage. You don't have to get it bang on
6 tbsp – just to about a quarter of its initial volume.

LEMON, LIMONCELLO AND TREACLE TART

This dish was inspired by a family trip to Sicily. The lemons were abundant in the garden, the limoncello abundant in the shops. It just needed something gooey.

The inside of a treacle tart is simple to knock together – you can do this stage in advance. The ice cream itself is quick and easy, and is not churned.

TREACLE MIX

zest and juice of 1 large unwaxed lemon

200 g/7 oz/¾ cup golden syrup

115 g/4 oz/2 cups white breadcrumbs

ICE CREAM

100 g/3½ oz/generous ½ cup icing sugar

70 g/2½ oz/¼ cup lemon curd

zest and juice of 1 large unwaxed lemon

4 tbsp limoncello

450 ml/16 fl oz/scant 2 cups double cream

NO CHURN MAKES 1 L

TREACLE MIX

1. Line a baking tray with baking parchment. Mix the lemon zest and juice with the golden syrup. Stir in the breadcrumbs. Depending on how dry the breadcrumbs are, you may need to add a little more syrup and lemon juice. The mixture should be pulpy, with no dry bits.

2. Spread out the treacle mix on the prepared baking tray and bake at 180°C/350°F/Gas mark 4 for about 15 minutes, until golden and crisping at the edges. Allow to cool completely.

ICE CREAM

1. Mix the icing sugar, lemon curd, lemon zest and juice and limoncello in a bowl. Refrigerate for 20 minutes for the flavours to develop. Then add the cream and whip to soft peaks.

2. Fold in the treacle mix pieces – they will be sticky, so break them up using your fingers. You might not want to use all the mix, but I have kept the quantities to those I use when I make it for myself – because if you're anything like me, some will get eaten along the way.

3. Transfer to a container and freeze overnight (there's no need to stir). Serve straight from the freezer.

WASSAIL CUP AND SPICED DIPPING STICKS

'Wassail' is an old English word meaning to cheer, or make merry with a drink – particularly warmed booze, either mulled beer or wine. It's a very convivial way to drink when you think about it – gripping hot mugs, huddled in groups to keep warm in Christmas markets. Let's bring back the expression: "What are you up to tonight? Off wassailing with the lads?"

This ice cream fills a 32-hole ice-cube tray. I have jumbo ice-cube trays – you might need two regular-sized ones. Silicone trays are brilliant, as the ices pop right out – you may struggle with regular plastic. If you don't have silicone trays, set the ice cream in a tub and serve a small scoop in each warm drink – an ice-cream float. You'll also need lolly sticks that fit upright in your freezer, and pretty glasses or teacups to serve. And, of course, friends to share with.

ICE CREAM

400 ml/14 fl oz/1¾ cups whole milk, plus extra to make a paste

400 ml/14 fl oz/1¾ cups double cream

½ tsp ground ginger

½ tsp ground cinnamon or 1 big stick of cinnamon

a few gratings of fresh nutmeg

1 tsp whole cloves

180 g/6 oz/¾ cup light brown muscovado sugar

3 tsp cornflour

a pinch of salt

MULLED WHITE WINE

2 unwaxed oranges

750 ml/25 fl oz bottle dry white wine

160 g/5½ oz/scant ⅔ cup light brown muscovado sugar

2 sprigs of fresh rosemary or fresh thyme

MAKES
32
STICKS

ICE CREAM

1. Pop the ice-cube tray into the freezer to chill, ready for the ice cream.

2. Warm the milk and cream in a saucepan with the spices and sugar, and leave to simmer and infuse for 5 minutes.

3. Make a paste with the cornflour and a splash of milk, then set aside. Strain the hot milk and cream into a bowl to remove the spice debris, then return to the pan (check first that the bottom of the pan is not scorched). Whisk in the cornflour paste, and continue to whisk until the custard has thickened. The custard is ready when you notice a change in consistency on the back of your spoon. Add a pinch of salt. Leave the custard to cool completely, then pop it into the fridge until completely cold.

4. Churn the ice cream in a machine, or stir-freeze, beating the ice cream with a fork every 30–40 minutes, until smooth but semi-frozen. Don't let it get too hard or you won't be able to spoon it into the ice-cube tray.

5. When the ice cream is churned to the desired consistency, remove the ice-cube tray from the freezer and use a teaspoon to fill each cavity with the ice cream.

6. Put the filled tray in the freezer for 30 minutes to firm up, then pop in the lolly sticks.

MULLED WHITE WINE

1. Pare the zest from the oranges, then juice them into a saucepan. Add the rest of the ingredients, plus 180 ml/6 fl oz/¾ cup of water, and warm through on a low heat. Don't boil the mulled wine; give it just enough heat for the sugar to dissolve and the orange zest to impart its flavour.

2. To serve, ladle into a jug decorated with fresh orange and herbs, or pour it straight into some teacups. Let your guests help themselves to the dipping sticks.

SLOE GIN FIZZ

If you want to experiment with dry ice as a means of freezing, this is the perfect recipe. When I first started playing with the stuff, I noticed that my ice cream had a slight fizzy taste. (If you can call it that – you know, like the difference between still and sparkling water.) It's thanks to the carbon dioxide trapped in the frozen mixture. You can't always detect it, but I noticed it most strongly in coffee flavours. Here, it's a bonus. You can, of course, churn this sorbet in a machine, or stir-freeze instead.

For further chat about dry-ice churning see page 12. Call around dry-ice suppliers – their minimum orders will differ. You'll need only a few cups for this and it must be food grade. I order my dry ice as small pellets, the size of rice grains.

For safety, it's important not to eat the ice cream until it is in a solid state. Before that point, as it bubbles, it will be extremely cold and you risk burning your mouth.

150 ml/5 fl oz/scant ⅔ cup sloe gin
160 g/5½ oz/scant 1 cup icing sugar
200 ml/7 fl oz/scant 1 cup tonic water
dry ice pellets

You will also need a large plastic bowl, or other non-heat-reactive bowl, and a pestle and mortar.

MAKES

0.5 L

1. Mix the sloe gin, icing sugar, tonic water and 120 ml/4 fl oz/½ cup of water by hand using a balloon whisk or a fork, until completely combined and the sugar has dissolved. Place in the large plastic bowl and put the bowl on top of a damp tea towel to secure it on the worktop.

2. The dry ice should be kept covered to avoid too much sublimation (dissolving into the air). When your sloe gin mixture is ready, take one cup of dry ice.

3. Crush the pellets to a powder in your pestle and mortar. Spoon the crushed dry ice into your sorbet mix, and stir it in with a metal whisk or fork. It will cloud up with gas, but you'll feel the mixture thicken.

4. Allow it to settle. If you've put in too much dry ice, the ice cream will be too hard to serve at this point (or even get out of the bowl), so let it soften in the fridge. If you're eating it straightaway, let it sit for 5 minutes to settle and stiffen. The ice cream will be at a safe temperature to eat when it has stopped fizzing.

You'll probably have had to order more dry ice than you need for this recipe, so make some other base mixes to freeze and marvel at your industrial amounts of ice cream, ready to celebrate birthdays galore. Better still, use the dry ice for a Gothic-themed party, with some bubbling witches' brew.

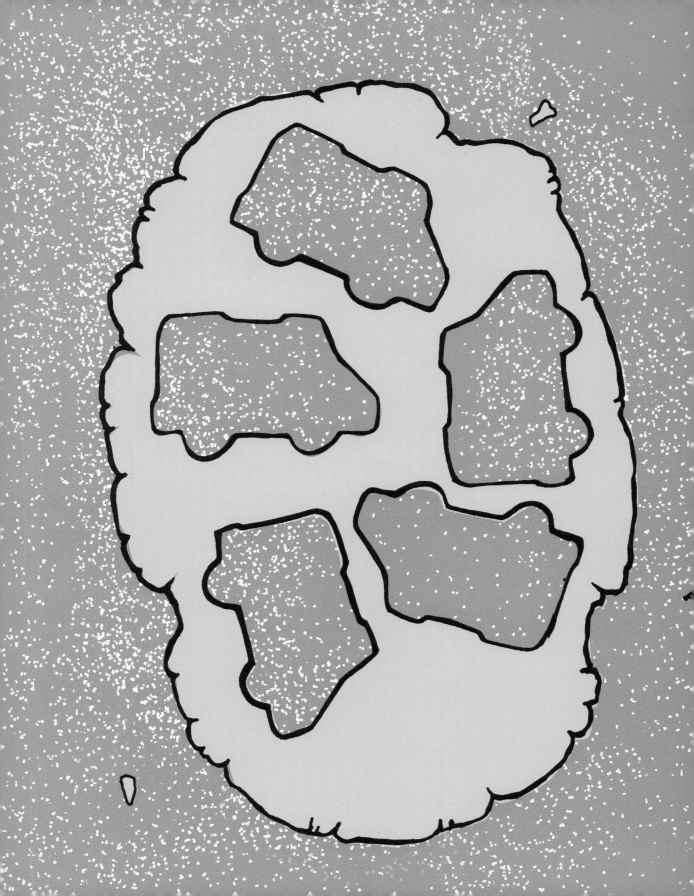

CRUNCHY

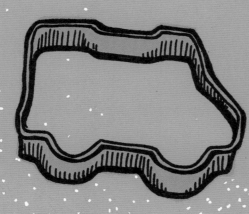

MARMALADE ON TOAST

This is a good morning ice cream. Many Sicilians eat their *gelato* for breakfast, stuffed into big, pillowy white bread rolls. I don't know why, but you can justify anything culinary if you can say the Italians do it. If you like, you can omit the toasted crumbs from the recipe and spoon the marmalade ice cream onto thick, buttered wholemeal toast.

The ice cream isn't churned. Instead, air is incorporated into the cream and meringue, so that the toast crumbs keep their bite.

This flavour won the 'Best Dessert' at the British Street Food Awards 2012, where Ginger's also scooped (pun intended) the 'Best of the Best' award.

100 g/3½ oz wholemeal bread
70 g/2½ oz/scant ⅓ cup soft dark brown sugar
2 large egg whites
1 tbsp icing sugar
400 g/14 oz Seville orange marmalade
350 ml/12 fl oz/1½ cups double cream

NO CHURN   MAKES   1 L

1. Heat the oven to 170°C/325°F/Gas mark 3. Then process the bread to make breadcrumbs. You want them quite coarse, so stop when they resemble rubble.

2. Spread the crumbs onto a baking tray and mix in the sugar. Bake for about 15 minutes until they are dry and crisp. Leave them to cool.

3. To make the meringue, whisk the egg whites in a scrupulously clean bowl. When they start to form soft peaks, add the icing sugar and continue to whisk for another minute until they turn glossy. Stop before the meringue becomes stiff.

4. Mix the marmalade into the double cream, then whisk the mixture into soft peaks. Again, stop before it becomes too firm, otherwise you won't be able to fold your mixtures together.

5. Fold together the meringue and marmalade cream. Use your largest bowl and a spatula, or a very big spoon. First, add a little of the meringue to the marmalade and cream, then add the rest into the bowl using a folding motion, turning the bowl as you go. The idea is to retain as much air as possible in the mix.

6. Scatter the crumbs over the top and repeat the folding and turning, mixing the crumbs evenly through the cream. Put the mixture in a tub, cover, and freeze overnight. This is easily scoopable almost straight from the freezer.

GRAND MEDAL OF MERIT VIENNA 18

JAMES KEILLER & SON'S

DUNDEE

MARMALADE

ONLY PRIZE MEDAL FOR MARMALADE

LONDON. 1262

HONEYCOMB AND ORANGE BLOSSOM

Buy the honeycomb candy if you like, but it's good fun to make. You add bicarbonate of soda to hot sugar to make it expand massively, creating the bubbles. It's my favourite chemical reaction in cooking – I get quite competitive with myself over how big I can make the bubbles. Some recipes add vinegar, which I find gives a more open, crispy texture but less of the toffee flavour.

Any nuggets buried in ice cream that need to retain a bite require the relative dryness of a whipped-cream base. Once you've made the honeycomb, this recipe is plain sailing.

HONEYCOMB

200 g/7 oz/generous ¾ cup sugar

4 tbsp golden syrup

1 tbsp cider vinegar or white wine vinegar (optional)

1 tbsp bicarbonate of soda

ICE-CREAM BASE

2 large egg whites

180 g/6 oz/generous 1 cup icing sugar

1½ tbsp orange blossom water

1 tbsp lemon juice

450 ml/16 fl oz/scant 2 cups double cream

NO CHURN

MAKES

1 L

HONEYCOMB

1. Line a baking tray with baking parchment, or use a silicone mat. Put 4 tbsp of cold water in a mug. Mix the sugar, golden syrup and vinegar (if using) in a heavy-based saucepan. Put this over a medium-low heat for 3–4 minutes. Allow the sugar to melt, then keep watching the pan – a sugary mass will bubble up. Using a spoon, drop a little of the mixture into the mug. If it's brittle (try biting it), it's ready; if it's still soft, give it another minute in the pan.

2. Turn off the heat and add the bicarbonate of soda quickly. Stir it through with a balloon whisk. The honeycomb will rise up; when it subsides, immediately turn it out onto the tray or mat and leave it to go completely cold, then chop it into bite-size shards. You won't use it all in the ice cream – the amounts here leave plenty to eat.

ICE-CREAM BASE

1. Whisk the egg whites to soft peaks, then set aside. In a large bowl, mix the icing sugar with the orange blossom water and lemon juice to form a paste.

2. Pour in the cream and whip until it forms soft peaks (taste when half whipped and add more blossom water, if necessary). Add one third of the egg whites and mix in vigorously with a fork. Spread the remaining egg whites on top and fold in with a spatula. Fold in the honeycomb rubble. Freeze the ice cream for at least 4 hours. There's no need to stir. Soften for 5 minutes in the fridge before serving.

PROPERMINT ICE CREAM

Proper = *adverb* (*-ly*) completely, thoroughly

Mint = *adjective* (*Mancunian dialect*) superlative, good, excellent

I've found discount stores are great places to pick up sweets and they have a plethora of inexpensive mint chocolates – those 'faux posh' brands are perfect for this.

1 large egg
4 large egg yolks
4 tbsp icing sugar
1 tsp cornflour
160 g/5½ oz/1 cup of any mixed mint sweets – try buttermints, mint balls, humbugs
300 ml/10 fl oz/1¼ cups double cream
After Eight chocolate mints, or other minty chocolates

NO CHURN   MAKES 1 L

1. Place a heatproof bowl over a pan of barely simmering water and add the whole egg and the yolks, sugar, cornflour and 2 tbsp of water. Whisk until pale and thick. Cool the mixture by placing the bowl in a larger bowl filled with ice-cold water.

2. Blitz the mixed mints in a food processor until you have powder and fine rubble. (I find that it's easier on my food processor if I put the mints in a bag and bash them with a rolling pin first.)

3. Whisk the cream into soft peaks and fold in the minty rubble. Pour in the cold egg mixture and fold it together well with a spatula.

4. If you've opted for After Eights, line a loaf tin with a double layer of cling film and spoon the ice-cream mix between layers of the chocolates, then, after freezing, cut the result as if it were a terrine, into slices. Otherwise, chop your chocolate mints coarsely and then fold them through the ice-cream mix. I've not specified a quantity – it's up to you to add however much you want. Transfer the mixture to a tub and freeze overnight; there is no need to churn or stir-freeze.

5. Before serving, soften in the fridge for 10 minutes.

LEMON, GINGER, GRAPE NUTS

Easy to make and with no need to churn, this ice cream is really good to put together with children. Grape nuts are a breakfast cereal made from wheat and barley. Containing neither grapes nor nuts, how did they get their name? The nibs resemble the seeds of grapes – a reasonable explanation. I'll accept that. They're quite unusual, with a delicious malty taste and fine gritty texture that stays hard in milk.

zest and juice of 1 unwaxed lemon
180 g/6 oz/generous 1 cup icing sugar
5 nuggets of stem ginger from a jar, chopped small, plus 2 tbsp of ginger syrup (or 130 g/4½ oz/½ cup of ginger preserve)
70 g/2½ oz/¼ cup lemon curd
2 large egg whites
350 ml/12 fl oz/1½ cups double cream
75 g/2½ oz/½ cup grape nuts cereal

1. Mix the lemon zest and juice in a bowl with 80 g/2½ oz/½ cup of the icing sugar, the pieces of stem ginger and the ginger syrup (or ginger preserve), and the lemon curd.

2. In a very clean bowl, whisk the egg whites until firm, then add half the remaining icing sugar. Whisk to combine and then tip in the rest of the icing sugar, whisking until you have a soft meringue – it doesn't need to be so firm that it stands in peaks.

3. Pour the cream into the lemon and ginger mix. Whip it together until you get soft peaks.

4. Spoon the meringue over the cream and fold it in. Sprinkle over the grape nuts and fold again to distribute them evenly, before transferring to a tub to freeze overnight.

5. This ice cream usually scoops straight from the freezer.

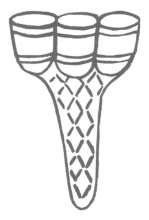

PLUM CRUMBLE

This makes an ice cream that you scoop, but it's very dessert-like, with big chunks of crunchy, buttery crumble going through it. I always have a seasonal fruit crumble on the menu – it says 'comfort food' like nothing else to the British public. You can use the topping recipe on any crumble you wish to bake. Make sure the butter is a decent salted variety, and maybe add a pinch of aromatic spice.

NO CHURN

MAKES 1.5 L

FRUIT COMPOTE

8 ripe plums

200 g/7 oz/generous ¾ cup sugar

juice of ½ a lemon

CRUMBLE

75 g/2½ oz salted butter, cubed

90 g/3¼ oz/¾ cup plain flour

90 g/3¼ oz/generous ⅓ cup sugar

40 g/1½ oz/½ cup porridge oats

MERINGUE

2 large egg whites

75 g/2½ oz/scant ½ cup icing sugar (unsifted)

350 ml/12 fl oz/1½ cups double cream

FRUIT COMPOTE

1. Preheat the oven to 180°C/350°F/Gas mark 4. The plums should be ripe enough to just rip out the stones. Then, roughly chop the flesh (skin on), mix it with the sugar and lemon juice and simmer on a medium-low heat for 15–20 minutes; just long enough to reduce slightly so the compote is not too watery. Leave the compote to cool, then taste it; add a dash of lemon juice if it's too sweet.

CRUMBLE

1. To make the crumble, work the cubed butter into the flour and sugar – if you like, use a food processor. When the mix resembles fine crumbs, rub in the oats by hand. Layer the crumbs on a baking tray or in a shallow ovenproof dish and bake until they are cooked to a biscuit colour, about 20 minutes. Allow to cool.

MERINGUE

1. Whisk the egg whites in a clean bowl until they're firm. Add all the icing sugar and continue whisking to a fairly thick meringue – just until the whisk leaves a trail. Set aside.

2. Whip the cream to soft peaks. Fold in the meringue, then the compote and finally the crumble pieces, in two big handfuls. Scoop into a tub and leave to freeze overnight. There is no need to stir during the freezing process.

3. Before serving, soften in the fridge for 5–10 minutes.

PASSION FRUIT WITH CHOCOLATE MERINGUE

Just typing the words 'passion fruit' makes my mouth water; adding chocolate to meringue makes it gorgeously cakey and gooey, but you still have a crisp shell.

PASSION FRUIT ICE CREAM

5 large or 10 small passion fruit

100 ml/3½ fl oz/½ cup whole milk

5 large egg yolks

180 g/6 oz/¾ cup sugar

300 ml/10 fl oz/1¼ cups double cream

CHOCOLATE MERINGUE

5 large egg whites

300 g/10½ oz/1¾ cups caster sugar

1 tsp cornflour

2 tbsp cocoa

40 g/1½ oz good-quality milk or dark chocolate, chopped

PASSION FRUIT ICE CREAM

1. Breaking up the passion fruit pulp in the following way adds to the flavour and leaves a little crunch from the seeds: scoop the insides of the passion fruit into a measuring jug. You should have about 200 ml/7 fl oz/scant 1 cup. Add enough milk to make 300 ml/10 fl oz/1¼ cups of liquid. Blend for 1 minute with a hand blender or food processor.

2. Mix the egg yolks and sugar in a saucepan. Strain the fruity liquid into the pan using a fine sieve. Some of the seed will get through, which is good. On a low heat, stir slowly for 5–10 minutes, until the mixture thickens into a custard. The custard is ready when you notice a change in consistency on the back of your spoon. Leave to cool.

3. When the custard is cold, stir in the cream. Churn it in a machine, or stir-freeze: put the tub in the freezer and every 30 minutes mash the frozen edges with a fork, until smooth and firm.

CHOCOLATE MERINGUE

1. Preheat the oven to 180°C/350°F/Gas mark 4. Line a baking tray with baking parchment. Whisk the eggs until they start to hold their shape. Add half the sugar and continue to whisk for 1 minute. Add the rest of the sugar and keep whisking until the mixture is a thick, glossy meringue. Add the cornflour and whisk it through.

2. Mix the cocoa and chopped chocolate in a bowl. Fold the chocolate mix quickly through the meringue with a spatula. Spoon 8–10 dollops onto the tray. Bake for 8–12 minutes on the middle shelf. Turn off the oven and leave the door ajar with the meringues inside, until just warm. Serve warm or cold with a scoop of ice cream on top.

MILK CHOCOLATE WITH SPICY BISCUITS

At a high-end restaurant in London I was offered the choice of having my dessert of chocolate moelleux made with either 45 % or 75 % cocoa-solids chocolate. It's a bold menu proposition – are you more adventurous for choosing the milk or the dark? The pressure! Good job I wasn't with one of those foodies who judge you on that kind of thing. I've used Maldon sea salt in these biscuits, plus an extra smidge sprinkled on each one. Szechuan pepper lends a warming spiciness against mild, comforting milk chocolate.

MAKES 1 L

MAKES 10–12 BISCUIT SANDWICHES

MILK CHOCOLATE ICE CREAM

300 ml/10 fl oz/1¼ cups whole milk
600 ml/20 fl oz/2½ cups double cream
180 g/6 oz/¾ cup sugar
3 tbsp cocoa
2 tbsp liquid glucose
200 g/7 oz good-quality milk chocolate, chopped

SPICY BISCUITS

130 g/4½ oz unsalted butter, softened
310 g/10½ oz/1¼ cups soft light brown sugar
2 large eggs
5 tsp Szechuan peppercorns
a pinch of Maldon sea salt
260 g/9½ oz/1¾ cups plain flour

MILK CHOCOLATE ICE CREAM

1. Bring the milk and cream to the boil in a saucepan, then turn down the heat. Mix the sugar and cocoa and spoon in the glucose on top. Tip into the pan and simmer for 5 minutes.

2. Turn off the heat and add the chopped chocolate. Let it melt for a minute before whisking into a smooth chocolate custard; leave to cool. Refrigerate. When chilled, churn in a machine, or stir-freeze, mashing with a fork every 30 minutes, until smooth and firm.

SPICY BISCUITS

1. Preheat the oven to 170°C/325°F/Gas mark 3. Combine the softened butter and the sugar with a fork. Briefly whisk the eggs. Whisk half the eggs into the sugar mixture; then the rest.

2. Grind the peppercorns with a generous pinch of the sea salt and stir into the mixture. Sift the flour into the bowl and stir to make a stiff batter. Chill in the fridge for 1 hour. Line a flat baking tray with baking parchment. Make little balls of chilled biscuit dough and flatten each with the palm of your hand. Sprinkle a few sea salt flakes over each biscuit. Bake for 20–25 minutes, until golden brown. (You may need to bake the biscuits in batches.)

3. To make the sandwiches, remove the ice cream from the freezer and soften in the fridge for 10 minutes. Mash it with a fork to make it pliable, then scoop or spoon it between the biscuits. Eat straightaway, or re-freeze to enjoy later.

ECCLES CAKE

This ice cream was specially created for the annual Salford Food and Drink Festival in the north of England. Much discussion was had as to whether the dish was, in fact, a Chorley cake ice cream – because you know the difference, right? Well, a Chorley cake has dried fruit going throughout the pastry, whereas its cousin from Eccles has the fruit just in the middle. Try as I might, I just couldn't get those pesky currants to sit still.

Either way, fruit soaked in cinnamon-spiced syrup and sugar-crusted flaky pastry made this a sell-out on the day.

A word of warning – you need to steep the fruit in the syrup for an hour before you start the rest of the recipe.

100 g/3½ oz/1 cup currants or raisins
4 tbsp sugar (any type)
4 tsp ground cinnamon
1 sheet of ready-made puff pastry
1 large egg, beaten
4–5 tbsp granulated sugar, for sprinkling
100 g/3½ oz/generous ½ cup icing sugar
250 ml/9 fl oz/1 cup double cream
4 tsp lemon juice

NO CHURN

MAKES

1 L

1. Put the dried fruit into a bowl and cover with the sugar and 3 tsp of cinnamon. Pour in enough freshly boiled water to just cover the fruit. Stir, then let it sit for an hour to soak.

2. Preheat the oven to 180–190°C/350–375°F/Gas mark 4–5.

3. Score the puff pastry sheet – I make 2.5 cm/1 in wide diamond shapes. Plenty of scoring helps you get lots of sugary crunchy bits. Brush the pastry with the beaten egg and sprinkle it generously with the granulated sugar, then bake it for 15 minutes until the pastry is risen and well browned. Watch it to check the sugar doesn't burn.

4. Remove the pastry from the oven and leave it to cool. Discard any pastry that isn't good and crunchy; it will be tasty, but too flabby for this ice cream.

5. Put the icing sugar into a large bowl with the remaining 1 tsp of cinnamon. Add the cream and lemon juice, and whip the mix to soft peaks.

6. Drain the fruit and fold into the cream. Crumble in the pastry, using as much or as little as you like. Fold again, then transfer to a tub and freeze overnight.

7. Before serving, soften at room temperature for 5–10 minutes.

ESPRESSO AMARETTO GRANITA

This is a fine post-dinner sharpener – maybe after a rich Italian dish, or heavy pasta carbs. It says: "Wake up y'all – pud's on the way …"

Disaronno is the most widely available brand of amaretto, but there are others. The flavour of bitter almonds comes purely from the kernels of apricot pits. Other brands use bitter almonds or a mixture of the two.

For each serving, put a few spoons in a shot glass or an espresso cup.

5 tbsp of your favourite ground coffee
600 ml/20 fl oz/generous 2½ cups freshly boiled water from a kettle
180 g/6 oz/¾ cup sugar
3 tbsp Disaronno amaretto liqueur

NO CHURN

MAKES

0.5+ L

1. Brew the coffee. Either steep in the freshly boiled water along with the sugar for 10 minutes then strain it through a fine sieve; or make it in a cafetière, but do add in the sugar.

2. Stir in the amaretto. Taste the blend for strength and sweetness. The more finely ground your coffee, the stronger the coffee flavour.

3. Freeze the mix in a good-sized tub that will give you a shallow depth of granita. Bring the granita out just once, after 20 minutes, and mash it up with a fork, then allow it to set in icy shards. Depending on your freezer, you'll need to leave it for anything from a few hours to overnight.

PEA AND MINT SORBET

Readily available in most shops and supermarkets, pea shoots are the green leaves from the pea plant. This is a sorbet best used in small amounts as a palate cleanser, or to complement a sweet dish – something field-fresh, such as strawberries with cream, or a strawberry tart.

70 g/2½ oz/scant ⅓ cup sugar

1 tbsp liquid glucose

50 g/1¾ oz/2 packed cups pea shoots

8–12 mint leaves

5 tbsp full-fat crème fraîche

a pinch of salt

juice of ½ a lemon

MAKES

0.5 L

1. Put the sugar and glucose with 400 ml/14 fl oz/1¾ cups of water in a saucepan. Bring to the boil to dissolve. Remove the pan from the heat and leave the syrup to cool.

2. When the syrup is cold, add the pea shoots and mint leaves to the pan and blitz with a hand blender or liquidiser until you get a smooth, bright green mix. Put the mixture through a fine sieve to remove any fibres.

3. Stir in the crème fraîche and taste. Season with a pinch of salt. Then add lemon juice a few drops at a time and taste. Keep adding lemon and tasting, taking care that you don't overpower the delicate flavours.

4. Leave the sorbet to go completely cold before churning in a machine, or stir-freeze: put the tub in your freezer, then every 30 minutes bring it out and mash the frozen edges with a fork, or use a hand blender to break up the ice crystals. You'll need to do this 3 or 4 times, until smooth and firm.

5. Before serving, soften in the fridge for 10 minutes.

Try rocket leaves and tarragon as a variation; substitute them for the pea shoots and mint, in the same quantities.

RHUBARB AND GINGER SORBET

You can't hear many foods. Not too many edibles make a sound, but rhubarb does. When it's force-grown in dark sheds, the stalks squeak into life. Does that make you think of Triffids?

A friend's recommendation of a restaurant once rested on the fact that you could hear the chips rustling in their baskets as the waiters passed by. Now I think about the sound of food.

5 stalks of rhubarb, about 4 cups when chopped

1 tsp ground ginger or 2 tsp finely grated root ginger

a splash of orange juice or water

110 g/4 oz/scant ½ cup sugar

3 tbsp liquid glucose or corn syrup

MAKES

0.75 L

1. Chop the rhubarb and simmer it gently in a saucepan with the ginger and a splash of orange juice or water. Let it collapse into a purée.

2. Meanwhile, place the sugar, 125 ml/4 fl oz/½ cup of water and the glucose or corn syrup in a small pan and heat gently until the sugar has dissolved. Then turn up the heat and boil the mix rapidly for 10 seconds. Remove from the heat.

3. Put the rhubarb into a bowl and slowly stir in the syrup. Use a hand blender or food processor to blitz until smooth, and set aside to cool. Once the mixture is cold, chill it in the fridge.

4. Churn the sorbet in a machine, or stir-freeze: put the tub in your freezer, then every 30 minutes bring it out and mash the frozen edges with a fork, or use a hand blender to break up the ice crystals. You'll need to do this 3 or 4 times, until smooth and firm.

5. Before serving, put into the fridge to soften for 10–15 minutes.

Try serving the sorbet in ice cups. Fill a balloon the way you would if you were making a water bomb, then blow a little extra air in on top. Tie the balloon, and put it in the freezer for around five hours. When you cut it open, it will be frozen on the outside and liquid inside. Tip away the extra water, and hey presto! Ice cups.

TEA GRANITA

Three things that disappoint me: deep-fried fast food, looking nostalgically at kids' TV shows, and herbal teas ... they seem brilliant, but really aren't. So what to do with all those promising-sounding and exotic tea bags taking up valuable cupboard space? Why, have churner, will churn!

Herbal tea granita makes a really lovely palate-cleanser. I don't bother with such things too often, but when friends are over for dinner and I'm doing lots of courses, this gives a nice touch.

I suggest redbush tea here because its tannin taste balances the sweetness, but I reckon any flavoured tea bag can work in this recipe. I also like a nice spiced chai granita. I have a brand of Aztec flavoured chai that uses cacao shells for a mild chocolate flavour, which is great too.

3 redbush tea bags
480 ml/17 fl oz/2 cups freshly boiled water from a kettle
8 tsp sugar
juice of ½ a lemon

NO CHURN   MAKES
0.5 L

1. Steep the tea bags in the freshly boiled water for 10 minutes. Remove them and then stir in the sugar. Leave to cool.

2. Add some fresh lemon juice to balance the flavour. If you've used a citrus-flavoured herbal tea bag, you might not need much juice, so taste as you go.

3. When the liquid is cold, pour it into a shallow container that will fit into a drawer in your freezer, and leave it there for 30 minutes. Remove from the freezer after this time and scrape around the sides where the ice has set. Repeat every 20 minutes or so. You might need to do this only a couple of times – a granita should be icy, unlike a sorbet or cream-based ice.

4. Before serving, leave to stand at room temperature for a few minutes, then bash it up and give each person a shot glass-sized amount.

GARDEN MINT AND CHOCOLATE CRISP

'Viennetta' ice creams were such a thrill when I was a kid; I've massive affection for them – and all mint and chocolate things in general. When you drizzle melted chocolate onto frozen ice cream it sets quickly, giving a crunch of thin chocolate. The Italians call this method *stracciatella*, meaning 'little threads'.

If you're not using a churner and are stir-freezing by hand, try it. You'll need a large surface area to form the *stracciatella* strands. Pouring melted chocolate into my super-duper ice-cream machine never works quite as well.

400 ml/14 fl oz/1¾ cups whole milk
400 ml/14 fl oz/1¾ cups double cream
a handful of mint leaves and stalks
6 large egg yolks
170 g/6 oz/scant ¾ cup sugar
170 g/6 oz good-quality milk or dark chocolate, chopped

MAKES

1 L

1. Start by making a classic custard base. Bring the milk and cream to a gentle boil; then add the mint. Let it simmer for 5 minutes. Give the milk a good stir from time to time to bruise the mint stalks so they release more flavour. In the meantime, beat the egg yolks with the sugar in a large bowl.

2. Suspend a fine sieve over the bowl containing the sugary yolks. Ladle through the warm milk and cream, straining to remove the mint. Lift up the sieve to stir the custard mix between each addition, until the flavoured milk mixture and eggs are fully combined. Pour the custard mixture into a clean pan, or the original pan as long as you haven't scorched the bottom.

3. Thicken the custard over a low heat. Keep stirring slowly so it doesn't catch on the bottom of the pan. The custard is ready when you notice a change in consistency on the back of your spoon. Remove the pan from the heat and give the mixture another good whisk, then leave it to cool completely.

4. When the custard is cold, churn in a machine, or if you are using the *stracciatella* method below, stir-freeze: put the tub in your freezer, then every 30 minutes mash the frozen edges with a fork or hand blender, until smooth and firm.

5. Before the ice cream hardens too much to spoon, melt the chocolate, either by microwaving it in short bursts or placing it in a heatproof bowl on a pan of very gently simmering water.

6. Let the melted chocolate cool until it is only hand hot, then spoon it in flicks and stripes over the ice cream. (Imagine you're Jackson Pollock!) You'll see that it hardens quickly. Turn the ice cream with a spoon, breaking up the strips of chocolate into shards, then drizzle again. Keep drizzling and turning until you've used up all the chocolate.

7. Soften the ice cream in the fridge for 10–15 minutes before serving.

CUCUMBER ICE CREAM

Cucumber is one of my most favourite smells. I can't put my finger on why it smells so great, being 90 % water, but melon and freshly cut grass spring to mind. Perhaps it's more the association with sandwiches in summer; cucumber brings out the flavour of good white bread and butter.

This ice cream is light and fragrant, but rich at the same time.

200 g/7 oz/scant ⅔ cup honey

400 ml/14 fl oz/1¾ cups double cream

550 g/1 lb 4 oz cucumber (about 1 large supermarket cucumber)

a pinch of Maldon sea salt flakes

juice of 1 lemon

MAKES

1 L

1. Combine the honey and cream in a saucepan and bring them to the boil, then simmer for 1 minute. Decant the sweetened cream into a bowl and give it a stir. Leave to cool.

2. Peel some of the cucumber – leave half the skin on to add some colour. Split the cucumber in half along its length and use a spoon to scrape away most of the watery core, then chop the cucumber into chunks. Blend the cream and cucumber together using a hand blender or food processor and then strain the mixture through a fine sieve. Taste and add a little sea salt and a little lemon juice if required.

3. When the mixture is completely cold, churn it in a machine, or stir-freeze: put the tub in your freezer, then every 30 minutes bring it out and mash the frozen edges with a fork, or use a hand blender to break up the ice crystals. You'll need to do this 3 or 4 times, until smooth and firm.

4. Before serving, soften in the fridge for 10 minutes.

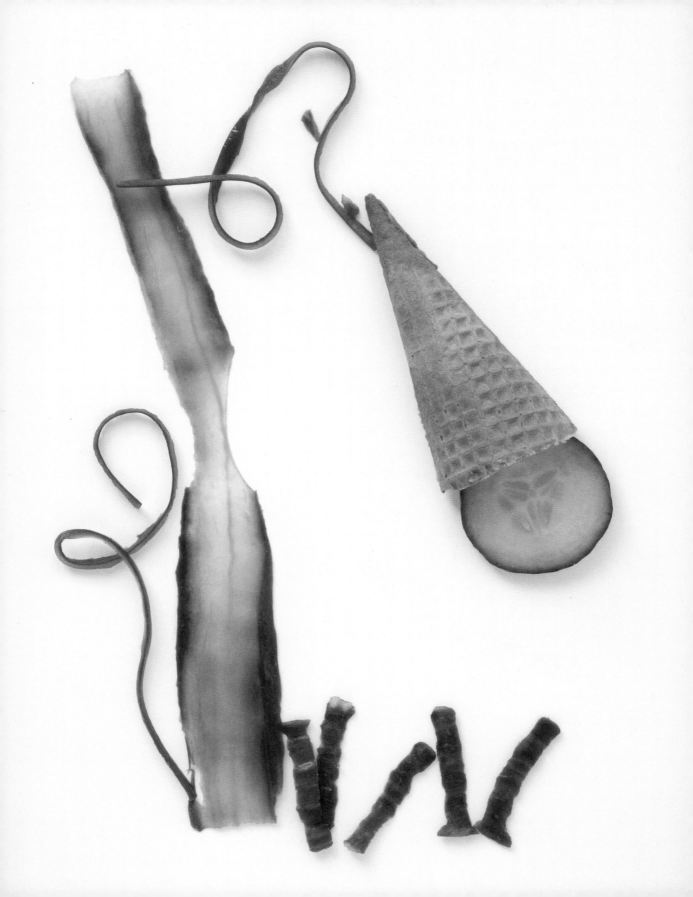

ORANGE, WATERCRESS AND TARRAGON SORBET

When I came back to this recipe to write it up for you, I found this random quote inserted: 'Without the element of uncertainty, the bringing off of even the greatest business triumph would be dull, routine, and eminently unsatisfying.'

I couldn't think why it was there … I thought back to how the recipe had come about. I had proffered this sorbet as my contribution to a high-end banquet, without having made it first to see whether it worked. The menus were printed before I knew it, and I spent a frantic week trying to make watercress and tarragon work together without tasting like a swamp.

I must have been Googling motivational quotes at the time – I certainly didn't make these wise words up. Anyway, this sorbet is peppery, spicy and refreshing. And worth the perseverance.

600 ml/20 fl oz/generous 2½ cups freshly squeezed orange juice
200 g/7 oz/generous ¾ cup sugar
6 bushy sprigs of fresh tarragon
2 large handfuls of fresh watercress
zest of 1 unwaxed orange

MAKES

1 L

1. Pour half the orange juice into a saucepan, add the sugar and bring to the boil. Stir until all the sugar has dissolved, then remove from the heat.

2. Tear up the tarragon and watercress and add to the pan, along with the orange zest. Give it a good stir and leave for 10 minutes for the flavours to infuse, with a lid on the pan.

3. Strain the liquid into a bowl using a fine sieve, and then add the rest of the orange juice. Leave to cool.

4. When cold, churn the sorbet in a machine, or stir-freeze: put the tub in your freezer, then every 30 minutes bring it out and mash the frozen edges with a fork, or use a hand blender to break up the ice crystals. You'll need to do this 3 or 4 times, until smooth and firm.

5. Before serving, soften in the fridge for 10–15 minutes.

This is a good dessert to eat after smoked fish – such as mackerel or salmon.

GIN AND BITTER LEMON SORBET

My mum's favourite drink – gin and bitter lemon. In the sorbet, the gin taste comes entirely from the juniper berries, but add a small splash of the hard stuff if you like. This is a nice pick-me-up between courses or after a barbecue. A little goes a long way.

1 unwaxed lemon

110 g/4 oz/scant ½ cup sugar

30 juniper berries, bruised

375 ml/12½ fl oz/generous 1½ cups carbonated bitter lemon

125 ml/4 fl oz/½ cup lemon juice

MAKES

1 L

1. Wash and chop the whole lemon, peel and all. Slices or smallish chunks are fine.

2. Put the lemon pieces, sugar and juniper berries in a saucepan with 250 ml/9 fl oz/1 cup of the bitter lemon and simmer for just 5 minutes, to avoid too much evaporation. Leave to cool completely.

3. Strain the cold liquid, then add the lemon juice and the rest of the bitter lemon. Churn in a machine, or stir-freeze: put the tub in your freezer, then every 30 minutes bring it out and mash the frozen edges with a fork, or use a hand blender to break up the ice crystals. You'll need to do this 3 or 4 times, until smooth and firm.

4. This sorbet is best eaten fairly soon after it's churned. However, if you've stored it for longer than a day, soften for 20–30 minutes in the fridge before serving.

GRAPEFRUIT POSSET AND WALNUT PRALINE

The excellent Aumbry restaurant in north Manchester has a most deceptively stunning dessert on its menu. I wouldn't have chosen it, left to my own devices, but it appeared on a tasting menu, and I was hooked – grapefruit posset with celery granita.

Don't get me wrong – I'm not a 'death-by-fudge/chocolate-oblivion' type of gal either, but grapefruit sounded way too austere for a dessert. I was wrong, wrong, wrong. I have a fight to persuade customers coming to my van to try this one – but disbelievers, trust me! Complex citrus flavours shine through the initial creaminess with a satisfying aftertaste.

GRAPEFRUIT POSSET

3 unwaxed pink grapefruits
165 g/6 oz/scant ¾ cup sugar
600 ml/20 fl oz/2½ cups double cream

WALNUT PRALINE

75 g/2½ oz/¾ cup walnuts, roughly chopped
100 g/3½ oz/generous ⅓ cup sugar

MAKES

1 L

GRAPEFRUIT POSSET

1. Zest one of the grapefruits straight into a saucepan. Juice all three into a jug to give around 400 ml/14 fl oz/1¾ cups of juice. Strain the juice into a bowl, discarding the pips. Reserve 2 tbsp of juice and put the remainder into the pan with the zest. Put it on a medium heat. Bring to a boil, then boil until reduced by half, about 15 minutes. Remove from the heat.

2. Add the sugar and cream to the pan, return to the heat and give the mixture a good whisk, then simmer for 3–4 minutes. Leave to cool completely, then stir in the reserved juice. Strain to remove zest bits, cool, and chill in the fridge.

3. Churn the posset in a machine, or stir-freeze: put the tub in your freezer, then every 30 minutes mash the frozen edges with a fork, until smooth and firm. The ice cream will need 5–10 minutes to soften before you serve.

WALNUT PRALINE

1. Lightly oil a sheet of baking parchment or use a silicone mat. Toast the chopped walnuts in a hot dry pan. Stop when you can smell their nutty aroma. Cover the nuts in an even layer of the sugar and let this caramelise on a medium heat until the sugar turns to a nice amber colour. Watch carefully – it happens quickly!

2. Tip the praline out onto the baking parchment or mat and leave to cool. Once cold, you can smash it into little shards, or fine rubble. Try wrapping it in a clean towel and smashing with a rolling pin. If you are rippling the praline pieces, scatter them over the just-churned or softly stir-frozen ice cream, and fold them through with a spatula. If you are using the praline as a decoration, scatter with the shards after scooping (see above).

If you can't find unwaxed grapefruits, buy waxed, then simply give them a scrub with warm soapy water, rinse well, and dry thoroughly.

FINGER FOOD

RHUBARB AND CUSTARD MACAROONS

I spent a year obsessing over French *macarons*. If ever a patisserie demanded accuracy in cooking, it's these – the delicate, crisp shell should give way to slightly chewy almond sponge, then a rich filling. In the oven, the domes should rise but not over-inflate and there should be a lifting that reveals the 'foot' or underside of the sponge.

My *macaron* odyssey ended in Paris, with a course given at the Alain Ducasse cookery school. The main thing I took away was to age the egg whites for as long as possible to avoid flat, overly chewy discs. See my tips, on page 152, for nailing the true French version, but if you want to be more slapdash, don't worry – yours won't look like the famous Ladurée *macarons*, but they will taste just as good.

If you can't wait to age the egg whites, my advice is to add an extra 45 g/1½ oz/ ½ cup of ground almonds – the results will be more cakey, but at least they won't be failed French *macarons*.

RHUBARB ICE CREAM

450 g/1 lb rhubarb, chopped

250 g/9 oz/generous 1 cup sugar

200 ml/7 fl oz/scant 1 cup whole milk

3 egg yolks

400 ml/14 fl oz/1¾ cups double cream

red food colouring (optional)

MACAROONS

225 g/8 oz/generous 1⅓ cups icing sugar, plus extra for the meringue mix

125 g/4½ oz/1 cup + 2 tbsp ground almonds

110 g/4 oz/about 4 egg whites, preferably aged

½ tsp vanilla extract

MAKES
10-12
MACAROONS

RHUBARB ICE CREAM

1. Sweat the rhubarb with the sugar and a tiny splash of water in a pan on a medium heat until the mixture is pulpy, about 10–15 minutes. If the fruit isn't as pink as you'd like, add a drop of food colouring. Pour the stewed rhubarb into a measuring jug – it should give you about 400 ml/14 fl oz/1¾ cups. Make it up to 600 ml/20 fl oz/2½ cups with the milk. Purée in a food processor or with a hand blender until smooth.

2. Break the egg whites into a clean, grease-free container and put them aside to use in the macaroons. Put 3 yolks into another bowl, or straight into a cold saucepan, and stir in the rhubarb mixture slowly. Place the pan over a low heat and stir until the custard has thickened. The custard is ready when you notice a change in consistency on the back of your spoon. Leave to cool completely, then whisk in the cream.

3. Churn in a machine, or stir-freeze: put the tub in your freezer, then every 30 minutes mash the frozen edges with a fork or hand blender, until smooth and firm.

MACAROONS

1. Preheat the oven to 150°C/300°F/Gas mark 2. Line two flat baking trays with baking parchment, or use silicone mats. Sift the icing sugar and ground almonds into a bowl.

2. In a separate bowl, beat the egg whites with a pinch of salt until they turn foamy, then add 30 g/1 oz/¼ cup of extra icing sugar. Whip to a stiff and glossy meringue.

3. Fold the icing sugar and almond mixture into the meringue in two batches, using a spatula or large spoon, and turning the bowl to help bring it all together. Add the vanilla extract and mix the batter more firmly until it leaves a trail that subsides in the mix when you lift the spatula.

4. Pipe 5 cm/2 in diameter circles onto the baking trays or silicone mats. Once you've piped the mounds, let them sit for 30 minutes at room temperature. This forms a skin that lifts in the oven, creating that 'foot'. Bake for 10–13 minutes, until the macaroons do not wobble to the touch.

5. Remove the macaroons from the oven but leave them on the trays to cool. When the macaroons are completely cold, use a palette knife or a sharp knife to lift them from the baking parchment or mats. It helps if you clean the knife between removing each one. Laborious I know, but I've found this to be the best way.

6. To serve, scoop ice cream between two little shells, sandwich-style.

7. One of the beauties of the macaroon is its freezeability. You can make them up and pop them back in the freezer for up to a week. They defrost quickly; serve when the ice cream is still firm but the icy edge has gone.

MY TIPS FOR THE ÜBER-MACAROON EXPERIENCE:

1. Sift the icing sugar with the ground almonds twice.

2. Use old egg white, not fresh – leave it out, covered, overnight or for two days.

3. Fold and mix the batter to the right consistency. Many people describe it as being like lava: wet but as firm as porridge; it will fall and leave a trail when you lift the spatula.

4. Keep the mounds that you pipe small and even. Start from a central point, letting the batter pipe outwards.

SUGAR PLUM, HONEY BUN, SWEET HEART!

Call them any of these adorable (or excruciatingly cheesy, depending on the status of your love life) monikers, these are delicate choux pastry buns, filled with fragrant, honeyed fruit ice cream. Choux pastry is a doddle to knock up. Then, just whip the ice-cream ingredients together, and pipe inside the risen batter. I've served these at wedding parties: the beauty of them is you can put them out for guests, and they'll defrost while holding their shape – completely and utterly delicious frozen, semi-frozen, or not frozen at all.

This recipe for choux pastry is from Prue Leith and Caroline Waldegrave's *Leith's Cookery Bible*. They say you won't go wrong if you follow it *exactly*, and I've never been brave enough to deviate. Oh, except for adding the fennel seeds ... no harm done.

CHOUX PASTRY BUNS

105 g/3¾ oz/¾ cup plain flour

a pinch of fine salt

85 g/3 oz unsalted butter

1 tsp fennel seeds, crushed

3 eggs

HONEY FRUIT ICE CREAM

juice of ½ large or 1 medium lemon

2 tbsp honey

5 or 6 prunes (about 50 g/1¾ oz)

3 or 4 dried figs (about 50 g/1¾ oz)

35 g/1¼ oz/⅓ cup whole almonds, either blanched or with their skins

75 g/2½ oz/¾ cup icing sugar, plus extra for dusting

300 ml/10 fl oz/1¼ cups double cream

NO CHURN MAKES 15 PIECES

CHOUX PASTRY BUNS

1. Preheat the oven to 200°C/400°F/Gas mark 6 and line 2 baking sheets with baking parchment. Sift the flour and salt together three times.

Put the butter, crushed fennel seeds and 220 ml/7½ fl oz/scant 1 cup of water into a saucepan, and bring to a rapid boil. Turn off the heat and immediately tip the flour into the pan, stirring vigorously with a wooden spoon until the batter is thick, almost like a dough. Leave this to cool on a plate.

2. When cool, put the batter in a bowl. Beat the eggs lightly with a fork and add to the batter a little at a time. Elbow power comes in handy here – beat until the batter has homogenised.

3. Use a dessert spoon to portion 15 balls across the 2 baking sheets. Bake for 20 minutes, or until risen and browned, about 20 minutes.

4. Take the choux buns from the oven, and cool them on a clean plate with plenty of space between them. Use a knife to prise the buns open where you intend to pipe the cream – slicing along an edge is fine. This allows steam to exit as they cool, making them as dry and crisp as possible.

HONEY FRUIT ICE CREAM

1. Combine the lemon juice and honey in a bowl. Chop the dried fruit and almonds as finely as you can, and add them to the bowl with the icing sugar. Give it all a good mix.

2. In a separate bowl, whisk the cream to soft peaks. Stir in the fruit and nuts to give a good, stiff mixture.

3. Use a piping bag to get the cream into the choux buns – plastic or paper ones that you snip the end from work best, but plastic sandwich bags work too. Pipe in enough to fill the holes, and freeze for at least 4 hours. Make sure you lay the buns on a tray with enough room between them to stop them freezing together.

4. Leave the buns to thaw for 10 minutes before eating. Serve dusted with a little icing sugar.

ENGLISH COUNTRY GARDEN SORBET POPS

To be honest, when I go into my back yard on a summer's day and inhale deeply, I get mainly diesel fumes, barbecues and a note of urban fox. But in this recipe I have a fantasy English country garden. So close your eyes, and let's all pretend we're in a Sunday-night BBC period drama.

This is a sorbet pop in two layers – rose, and cucumber, honey and mint. You'll need an ice-cube tray and some lolly sticks. Alternatively, you could set the layers in actual lolly moulds. Either way, get the moulds nice and cold by putting them into the freezer first – this will give you more time to work with the sorbet. Don't forget to allow enough height for the sticks.

MAKES

20–25 POPS

ROSE LAYER

85 g/3 oz/⅓ cup sugar

2 level tbsp liquid glucose

1 tbsp rose water

1 tsp rose syrup or a little pink food colouring

1 tbsp lemon juice

CUCUMBER LAYER

100 g/3½ oz/scant ⅓ cup honey, runny or set

2 tbsp liquid glucose

250 g/9 oz cucumber

1 large sprig of mint, leaves picked

2½ tbsp gin (optional)

a pinch of Maldon sea salt

4 tbsp soured cream

1½ tbsp lemon juice

ROSE LAYER

1. In a small pan, bring the sugar and glucose, plus 125 ml/4 fl oz/½ cup of water to the boil, then turn off the heat. Add an additional 125 ml/4 fl oz/½ cup of water to the pan, along with the rose water, syrup and lemon juice. Have a taste – rose water brands vary a lot in strength, so add more if the mixture needs it. Leave to go cold.

2. Churn in a machine. Once churned, put a teaspoon of the sorbet into the bottom of each of your moulds and then pop the tray back into the freezer.

CUCUMBER LAYER

1. Put the honey and glucose in a saucepan with 125 ml/4 fl oz/½ cup of water. Bring to the boil (don't let it go any further), then turn off the heat. Peel half the cucumber, deseed it and chop it up. Use a hand blender or food processor to blitz it with the mint, gin (if using), sea salt and honey syrup. Stir in the soured cream and lemon juice and leave the mixture to go completely cold. Taste – does it need more lemon to balance the sweetness?

2. Once the rose layer is in the freezing moulds, churn the cucumber sorbet in a machine. When it's done, spoon it on top of the rose layer, then push a lolly stick into each one. If they feel too soft to hold the sticks upright, just pop them into the freezer and try again in 30 minutes or so. Freeze for at least 4 hours before serving.

ETON MESS BARS

I'd been serving Eton Mess from the van one day (I'd run out/needed a break from ice cream), and had some mixed ingredients left over in a bowl. I put the bowl in the van's freezer, just until I got back home – and this was the result ... a happy accident.

Traditionally, Eton Mess uses strawberries, but here we're using raspberries.

150 g/5 oz/1¼ cups fresh raspberries
4 tbsp icing sugar
lemon juice
270 ml/9½ fl oz/scant 1¼ cups double cream
8 meringue nests

NO CHURN

MAKES 10–12 PIECES

1. Line an 18 cm/7 in or 20 cm/8 in square cake tin with baking parchment.

2. Gently mash the raspberries and icing sugar with a little lemon juice in a bowl. Whisk the cream to fairly stiff peaks and crumble six of the meringue nests over the top. Tip the raspberry mixture into the cream and then roughly fold everything together with a spatula or spoon.

3. Spread the mixture evenly into your cake tin, and crumble the last two meringue nests on top, pressing the pieces in slightly.

4. Freeze for at least 3 hours. Then cut the frozen slab into bars to serve.

CHOCOLATE EASTER EGGS

A fun, alternative gift at Easter: real eggshells filled with chocolate ice cream.

Once the shell is broken with a few taps or a firm roll along a tabletop, it peels away easily, because the inner membrane stays intact. You're left with a smooth ice-cream egg – but it does melt, so get it down you!

This idea came from a brainstorming session with fellow chef Rob Owen Brown from Manchester's The Mark Addy restaurant. Rob was hosting a sensual eating event and wanted to use ice cream in an innovative way. With diners blindfolded, they were first to feel the egg, then realise that the goods were hidden inside. Good job they couldn't see what a mess they were getting in.

12 large eggs (and the carton)
1 litre/35 fl oz Chocolate ice cream (page 21) or Chocolate, Red Wine, Clove and Black Pepper ice cream (page 102)

MAKES

12

EGGS

1. First hollow the eggs. To do this give the eggs a light wash with warm water and soap. When they're dry, very gently tap the narrow end of each egg on a hard surface to dent the shell. Hold the egg upright and pick away a penny-sized circle from the broken area.

2. Now, turn the egg upside down over a bowl and give it a gentle shake, you might be lucky enough to see the whole egg come out, yolk intact. (Use the yolks to make the Chocolate, Red Wine, Clove and Black Pepper ice cream.) No worries if any of the yolks break into the white albumen – there's always scrambled egg for breakfast tomorrow. Repeat for all the eggs, each time sitting the eggshell, open end up, back in the egg carton. When all the eggs are hollowed out, put the filled carton in the freezer.

3. Whether you've churned your chosen ice cream, or used the stir-freeze method, it needs to be spoonable – don't store it in the freezer once it has churned to a soft consistency.

4. Bring out the shells from the freezer when they're good and cold. Take a teaspoon and fill each egg with ice cream. Wipe the shells with a damp cloth if any ice cream spills. Pop the eggs back into the carton, and then put the whole lot into the freezer to harden for at least 3 hours before you give them out.

Try a mix of brown, white and blue hens' eggs. They look sweet all together in a box. I've used all blue here and decorated the tops with candy letters, but you could decorate with edible glitter too.

SUPPORTING CAST

FRENCH ELVIS
FRENCH TOAST WITH SALTED CARAMEL AND PEANUT BUTTER ICE CREAM

To the discerning, The King is known less as a rocker than as a true *artiste* of the sandwich. This sweet and salt sensation, is, naturally, named for him.

MAKES
2
SANDWICHES

FRENCH TOAST

2 large eggs

4 tsp sugar

125 ml/4 fl oz/½ cup milk or
  single cream

2 very thick slices of white bread

a good knob of butter (salted or unsalted)

TO SERVE AS A FRENCH ELVIS

2 bananas, sliced

Peanut Butter and Salted Caramel ice
  cream (page 75)

strawberry jam, to taste

FRENCH TOAST

1. Beat the eggs and sugar into the milk or cream in a bowl. Dip your bread doorsteps into this thin batter, letting them soak briefly. Meanwhile, melt the butter in a frying pan over a medium–low heat.

2. Fry the eggy bread for 3–4 minutes on each side until golden.

FRENCH ELVIS

1. Let the slices cool enough for you to be able to hold each one as you slice each lengthways across the crust, into the soft interior of the toast, to make a pocket. Arrange the slices of banana, with the ice cream and a slick of jam, inside the pocket of each slice – and get stuck in before the ice cream melts!

ROASTED FRUIT

Feel free to improvise with the fruit.
I use plums, peaches, bananas, pineapple,
apple, figs. But the choice is yours …

SERVES

2

4–6 pieces of fruit, to taste
1 vanilla pod
3 tbsp demerara sugar (or to taste)
30 g/1 oz unsalted butter, cubed
ice cream, to serve

1. Preheat your oven to its highest setting and line a baking tray with baking parchment.
   Cut the fruit into largeish chunks. Scrape the seeds from the vanilla pod, then mash them
   about with the sugar in a bowl.

2. Toss the fruit with the sugar mix to give it an even coating. Spread out the fruit chunks on
   the baking tray. Dot little cubes of the butter over the top. Bake for 10–15 minutes.

3. Serve with any ice cream. My choice would be Honey and Tahini (page 65).

POP TARTLETS

Spring roll pastry is widely available in
larger supermarkets and Asian grocers,
usually in the frozen section. You can use
filo pastry instead, but it's thinner, so if you
do, use two sheets together, each brushed
with a little melted butter.

8 sheets of spring roll pastry
8 tbsp jam – any flavour you like
1 large egg, lightly beaten

MAKES

8

TARTS

1. Preheat the oven to 180°C/350°F/Gas mark 4. Line a baking tray with baking parchment.
   Put each pastry sheet flat on your worktop. Blob 1 tbsp of jam in the centre of each square.

2. Bring the top third of each sheet down over the jam, then fold the bottom third up over this.
   Press the jam a little to spread it out. Flip the tart over, and brush this side lightly with
   the beaten egg. Now bring the two side edges in to make a square. Repeat for all the pastry
   squares, then put all eight onto the baking tray and use any leftover egg to brush the tops.

3. Bake for 7–8 minutes, or until crisp. Let the tarts cool for 5 minutes once out of the oven,
   then dust them with icing sugar while they're still warm and serve with an ice cream of
   your choice. Chocolate (page 21) or Guinness and Gingerbread (page 106) work splendidly.

EASY DOUGHNUTS

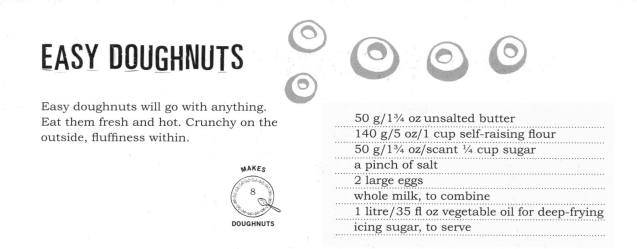

Easy doughnuts will go with anything. Eat them fresh and hot. Crunchy on the outside, fluffiness within.

MAKES
8
DOUGHNUTS

50 g/1¾ oz unsalted butter
140 g/5 oz/1 cup self-raising flour
50 g/1¾ oz/scant ¼ cup sugar
a pinch of salt
2 large eggs
whole milk, to combine
1 litre/35 fl oz vegetable oil for deep-frying
icing sugar, to serve

1. In a bowl, rub the butter into the flour so it resembles coarse breadcrumbs. Mix in the sugar and a pinch of salt. Beat the eggs a little and mix them into the dough until smooth, then add enough milk to give the dough a dropping consistency.

2. Pour the oil into a large saucepan so that it reaches only a third of the way up the sides. Heat the oil on a medium–high heat. To test if it's hot enough, drop in a crumb of bread. If it sizzles, the oil is ready. Drop a tablespoon of the batter into the hot oil, and fry until golden all over. Repeat, a tablespoon at a time, with the remaining batter. Serve the doughnuts with a dredging of icing sugar.

OMELETTE SOUFFLÉS

A more refined version of everyday omelettes, good with any ice cream – but particularly the fruity ones – these fluffy soufflés are the taste equivalent of a kiss.

MAKES
4
SOUFFLÉS

4 large eggs
4 tsp sugar
a knob of butter (salted or unsalted)
ice cream, to serve

1. Separate the eggs, making sure the whites go into a perfectly clean bowl. Whisk the whites to soft peaks. In another bowl, whisk the sugar into the yolks until pale and slightly thickened. Fold the whites into the yolk mix, adding a little at a time.

2. Melt the butter in a frying pan over a low heat, then use a large serving spoon to spoon in the yellow clouds of mixture, two at a time. Give them just 1–2 minutes on each side.

BASIC WAFFLES

Quick and easy, these American-style waffles are dense and fluffy pillows, cooked in a frying pan with a little butter. This recipe makes eight, so if there's just one or two of you, halve the quantities.

MAKES
8
WAFFLES

300 g/10 oz/2 cups self-raising flour
4 tbsp caster sugar
½ tsp salt
250 ml/9 fl oz/1 cup whole milk
2 large eggs
25 g/1 oz unsalted butter

1. Sift the flour into a large bowl and add the sugar and salt.

2. Put the milk into a jug, then break in the eggs, mixing with a fork.

3. Pour the milk and egg mixture into the flour bowl, a little at a time, beating until you have a thick glossy batter with no visible lumps.

4. Over a fairly low heat, melt the butter in a frying pan. Using a serving spoon, put dollops of the batter into the pan. (I cook four at a time, but the size of your waffles is up to you.) They take about 4 minutes each; flip them halfway through the frying.

5. Serve these versatile little beauties with any flavour ice cream.

PEANUT BUTTER SAUCE

I stand by my assertion that peanut butter goes with everything, so what better sauce recipe?! I use smooth peanut butter, but go crunchy by all means.

MAKES
0.2 L
SAUCE

15 g/½ oz unsalted butter
3 tbsp sugar
100 g/3½ oz/½ cup peanut butter
1 heaped tbsp full-fat natural yogurt or crème fraîche
a pinch of salt

1. Bring 125 ml/4 fl oz/½ cup of water to a gentle boil in a saucepan with the butter and sugar. Boil for about 1 minute, then turn off the heat and blend in the peanut butter with a balloon whisk.

2. Stir in the natural yogurt or crème fraîche with a pinch of salt. Serve warm over ice cream.

STOCKISTS

Most ingredients used in this book can be found in any well-stocked supermarket these days. But if not, try these online sources.

CAMEL'S MILK

camelmilkuk.net
– for UK availability

CHESTNUTS (COOKED)

melburyandappleton.co.uk

DURIAN FRUIT

hoohing.com
– national store locator

GRAPE MOLASSES

webstore.ottolenghi.co.uk

GRAPE NUTS

steenbergs.co.uk

GRAPPA

thedrinkshop.com

HALVA

hollandandbarrett.com

HELLENIC EXTRA VIRGIN OLIVE OIL

goodnessdirect.co.uk

JOSTABERRIES

unwins.co.uk
– seeds and bushes

LIQUORICE ROOT

healthysupplies.co.uk

LOCAL HONEY PRODUCERS

beedata.com

MALT GRAIN

quaffale.org.uk or
barleybottom.com

MASTIC

steenbergs.co.uk

ORANGE BLOSSOM WATER

theasiancookshop.co.uk

PINK PEPPERCORNS

steenbergs.co.uk

ROSE WATER AND SYRUP

steenbergs.co.uk

SLOE GIN

thedrinkshop.com

TAHINI

equalexchange.co.uk

TAMARIND PASTE

melburyandappleton.co.uk

VANILLA EXTRACT

healthysupplies.co.uk

VANILLA PODS

vanillatoyou.com

WHITE TRUFFLE OIL

trufflehunter.co.uk

GINGER'S
COMFORT EMPORIUM

INDEX

GLOSSARY OF UK AND US TERMS

UK	US
baking tray	cookie sheet
barbecue	grill
biscuit	cookie
caster sugar	superfine sugar
cornflour	cornstarch
double cream	heavy cream
filo pastry	phyllo pastry
frying pan	skillet
golden syrup	light corn syrup
grated	shredded
greaseproof paper	waxed paper
hob	range
ice lolly	popsicle
icing sugar	powdered sugar
jam	preserves or jelly
dark chocolate	bittersweet chocolate

UK	US
plain flour	all-purpose flour
pudding	dessert
self-raising flour	self-rising flour
single cream	light cream
sorbet	sherbet
stone (of fruit)	pit
sultanas	golden raisins
sweets	candy
tea towel	kitchen towel
treacle	molasses
vanilla pod	vanilla bean

ACKNOWLEDGEMENTS

The author would like to thank

Caroline Harris and Clive Wilson; Nicky Hill and all
at Simon & Schuster; and Francine Lawrence,
Emily Dennison, Anita Mangan, Abigail Read, Eirlys
Penn, Judy Barratt, Georgina Harris, Jane Middleton,
Peter Sargent, Edward and Kate Kelsey, Jenni Moore,
Susanna Amato, Vic McLynn, Daniel Manicolo,
Nicky Hancock, Katie Popperwell, Rachel Davies,
Henrietta Smith-Rolla, Ailsa McLaggan, Greg Walsh,
Stan Chow, Tom Sheehy, Kara Johnston,
Emma and Lucie Unsworth, Irshad Ashraf,
Alix Walker, Andy Boughton, Ben Pryce, Nula Mathers,
Gonzalo Fernandez Mardomingo Gonzalo,
Georgios Tzimas and John Matthews.

Thank you also to The Marble Brewery, The English
Rose Bakery, On The Corner Cafe,
www.lowbros.de, mrgauky.com, mrpenfold.com and
aplacecalledcommon.co.uk.